Prenup

Postnup

How They Work
and Why You Might
Need One

Richard G. Kent

ISBN: 1-4392-3140-0
ISBN-13: 9781439231401

Visit www.booksurge.com to order additional copies.

Foreword

Premarital agreements are widely misunderstood creatures. Very few people and very few lawyers understand what they really are, how they work, why they don't work, or why you might need one. Richard Kent's book breaks down the myths and explains the facts surrounding premarital agreements.

This book is a must read if one is contemplating either getting into or getting out of a premarital agreement, or if one is simply curious about the unique notion of preparing in advance for one's divorce as one enters into marriage.

To some people, a premarital agreement is a four letter word, to others, a necessity. Whatever your beliefs about them are, the question arises, if you have one, why aren't you safe from the painful litigation associated with the dissolution of a marriage? Kent's book provides the answer.

There is a need for Kent's book because there is a void in matrimonial law on the subject of premarital agreements. Kent, long recognized as a leading expert in the area of matrimonial law, has written the definitive work on premarital agreements. His book is a lively, engaging, helpful read for both the layperson and the lawyer. It is both practical and scholarly.

After reading Kent's book, you will understand what a premarital agreement is, what it can and cannot do, and whether yours is arguably enforceable or unenforceable.

One no longer needs to contemplate premarital agreements in the dark. Kent's book sheds light on a widely misunderstood subject and breaks it down with refreshing clarity.

Susan F. Filan

MSNBC Senior Legal Analyst

Former CT prosecutor

Preface

The idea for this book came to me after I had dinner in 2007 with an investment banker from Greenwich, Connecticut. He indicated to me that many hedge funds in Fairfield County, Connecticut and in New York City are requiring their partners without prenuptial agreements to enter into postnuptial agreements so that their spouse would not have an interest in the hedge fund in the event of a divorce. They are also requiring partners who are about to marry to enter into prenuptial agreements.

This was interesting and I got to thinking about my law practice and how many more prenuptials I had put together in 2007 than in 2006. Normally I had been writing about 5 or 6 prenuptials a year and the number had doubled in 2007. I had been writing very few if any postnuptial agreements. This year I have gotten a number of calls with respect to writing post-nuptial agreements.

An interesting dynamic is whom were coming to see me about prenuptials and occasionally about postnuptials.

Early on in my practice in the late 1970's, I had been meeting with people entering second marriages who had substantial assets that they wanted to protect.

In 2007 I found myself meeting with a whole variety of people. I found myself meeting with people who were entering into domestic partnerships and not marriages, young people entering into a first marriage who had interests in trusts to protect, people entering into third or fourth marriages and people who really didn't have a good reason for entering into a prenuptial but felt that it was the thing to do in 2007.

Matrimonial law is clearly replete with trends. The early 1990's saw the men's revolution in custody cases. That is a situation in which more men were getting custody than ever before. In the 1970's, when I started practicing law men very infrequently got custody. But in the early to mid 1990's in over 60% of contested custody cases which only comprise of 9% of all custody cases men have ended up getting custody. This was followed by a trend in which many men were accused of sexually abusing their children by their soon to be former wives in an effort to stave off the custody claim.

The early 2000's saw many more cases of split custody in which kids would live with one parent for one week and the other parent for the other week.

As this decade draws to a close the trend that I have been seeing most prevalently relates to prenuptials and postnuptials and living together agreements and I expect this trend to further burgeon as the decade draws to an end as more and more people find out about the documents and recognize that they are well suited for their marriage. There is also an implicit recognition that marriage is an imperfect institution and that such documents are not frowned upon.

Implicit in all of the prenuptials and postnuptials is a terse recognition that marriages do come to an end and aren't necessarily forever. The divorce rate now hovers around 50% or perhaps a little less, but that also includes second and third marriages which have a higher incidence of divorce. Actually some studies indicate that divorce is waning and in bad economic times such as these that is the trend that I have seen over the years in my law practice. Court filings in the month of January 2009 in the State of Connecticut were way down from filings in January of 2008.

I wrote this book for a number of reasons. First and foremost it is topical. I have found over the past 3 years or so that more and more people are coming into my office to put together prenuptial agreements and some have an interest in postnuptial agreements. I started practicing law in 1975 and if I wrote one prenuptial a year for the first 5 years of my practice it was a lot. That trend continued through the 1980's and it really wasn't until the 1990's with the proliferation of information about prenuptials and especially celebrity divorces on the national level that clients started to come in with rapidity to get prenuptials completed.

I have spoken with a number of matrimonial lawyers in Connecticut, New York and California and all have had the same experience.

My theory is that with the dramatic shifting of wealth from one generation to another there is a concern articulated by parents that their children not enter into marriage without some financial protection. The same is true on the other end of the spectrum as it relates to older individuals whose children urge them either for selfish financial reasons or out of caring that their parent needs to be protected with a prenuptial agreement in a second marriage.

This book obviously required the assistance of a number of individuals.

First and foremost I would like to thank my friend Attorney Raoul Felder from New York. I am happy to call him both a friend and a colleague. His invaluable assistance to me by recounting numerous prenuptials anecdotes has been quite important. I want to thank Attorney Michael Meyers, my law partner and a member of Best Lawyers in America. He has given me a tremendous amount of insight into the prenuptial process.

Attorney Mark Soboslai has also been helpful as he was the architect of one of the leading prenuptial decisions in the State of Connecticut, <u>Dornemann v. Dornemann</u>. Mark has insight, intelligence and compassion as a family lawyer and was always willing to discuss not only his case but other cases while I was preparing this book.

Attorney Alexandra Leichter from California, who I have never met personally but have spent much time emailing has helped me a great deal with the prenuptial concepts as it relates to Jewish divorces and Gets. She is an expert in Orthodox Jewish law especially as it relates to matrimonial matters.

My stepdaughter, Beth Kasden, a legal marketer helped bring many issues to the fore with the author prior to the book being put together.

There are a number of lawyers whose wisdom and insight has helped me along the years. In that regard I want to thank Attorneys Ed Kweskin, Ed Walsh, Alex Breiner and a host of others.

The author also owes a debt of gratitude to the many judges before whom he has appeared and helped him to shape his legal career. Those include in no special order Judge Stanley Novick, Judge Mary Louise Scofield, Judge Larry Hauser, Judge Elaine Gordon, Judge Fred Freedman, the late Judge Edgar W. Bassick, III, Judge Barry Pinkus, and Judge Patty Pittman.

This book could not have been written without the cooperation and assistance of my legal assistant Lori Schrager whose insights and life experiences proved invaluable to me.

Last but not least I would like to thank my family members and especially my wife Lisa, also an attorney who has been extremely giving in her time as it relates to the compilation and arduous work involved in putting together a book of this magnitude. By the way, she and I do not have a prenuptial agreement.

I would like to say thank you to all of you.

Table of Contents

Chapter I
The Commitment Conversations

The Equality in Marriage Institute located in New York, www.equalityinmarriage.org has come up with a document known as the commitment conversation which relates to a guide to the most important discussions for couples who are about to marry or who are already married. Many elements of the commitment conversation are applicable to the discussions that couples should have either before the marriage regarding a prenuptial agreement or during the marriage regarding a postnuptial agreement.

The conversation obviously has as its predicate the word trust. It involves a willingness on the part of both parties to invest the necessary time and energy to make sure that they build and maintain a strong partnership and don't erode the partnership by virtue of discussions regarding or time spent in negotiating and executing a prenuptial or postnuptial agreement. Before parties even discuss either of those elements they need to understand the legal ramifications of marriage and educate themselves either individually or collectively to the legal commitment they are making.

Communication is the key element not only to a marriage but to discussions regarding a prenuptial or postnuptial agreement.

Communication is a tricky element. There is no right or wrong way to communicate with a prospective spouse or a spouse.

The Institute has set forth a number of points regarding communication and they seem worthy of repeating here:

- Make sure your body language, facial expressions and voice tones are in line with your message.

- Try and be positive when bringing up concerns you may have. It helps to start out by talking about positive things and then moving into the deeper discussions and problem areas.

- Compromise is an essential tool in this process.

- If you can't come up with a definitive solution at least try to end the conversation on the topic on a positive note.

- Feel free to use the time out card if the discussion gets too intense. If an argument gets heated and irrational it is better to postpone the discussion to a later time and place.

- Realize when you need outside help to communicate effectively. If the prenuptial or postnuptial is better served in a psychologist's office, with a third party friend present or in front of lawyers then do it there. This is more of a subjective than objective determination.

When it is time to have the prenuptial or postnuptial discussion be sure that you have given yourself a block of uninterrupted time to have the discussion. Don't do it 15 minutes before going to work in the morning, on the telephone or just before you go to bed.

It is impossible to have this discussion without first discussing finances and perhaps even having financial affidavit forms or financial worksheets completed. Those forms can be obtained from Attorneys or on line.

Each party should pull out their respective paperwork and share with their partner their current financial status which includes but is not limited to expectancies of immediate or future inheritances.

For parties who decide to live together, as opposed to marrying and hence not entering into a prenuptial agreement, a living together agreement which parallels much of the language which would be set forth in a prenuptial agreement has been recognized in many jurisdictions throughout the country as an enforceable contract in a civil court, as opposed to a matrimonial or family court. This would take more time to enforce, but would still have the indicia of validity.

Years ago, non marital cohabitation was rare due to the mores of society. Also at the time common law marriage was regulated in most states by marital laws.

Interestingly, family law certainly sanctioned business contracts and provided certain equitable relief for cohabitants in the 1950's and 1960's but no legal rights were created given the fact that courts viewed non-marital cohabitation as being socially undesirable.

Chapter 2
The Cost of a Prenuptial

The author practices law in Fairfield County, Connecticut where divorces can range in price anywhere from $50,000 to $300,000, depending largely on whether or not the case in question is a fully contested custody case. A recent case in the Middletown, Connecticut courts called for combined legal fees of in excess of 4 million dollars. This is a large price to pay especially when a valid prenuptial agreement can save the parties all or most of those exorbitant legal fees.

Even though they perform a valuable function, prospective clients always must make a determination as to whether or not the cost of the lawyer, which sometimes can be in excess of a year or more of college education for a minor child is worth it in the long run.

This is not to say that lawyers are not necessary in matrimonial cases and specifically matrimonial cases which include massive amounts of income and assets and custody issues. What is meant, is that the prospective legal fees can often times be avoided with a validly executed and fluid prenuptial agreement.

One problem that is obviously raised by this analysis is that prenuptial agreements can rarely if ever deal with issues which impact on children, except in some cases with respect to child support. A question which must be asked is whether or not custody is going to be at issue. If so, a prenuptial agreement is probably not worth the paper that it is written on. The answer from most matrimonial practitioners is a resounding yes.

The above answer leads to a discussion of the concept of bifurcation. Courts in most jurisdictions are willing to bifurcate finances from custody. Thus, if a validly executed prenuptial agreement can solve the issue of finances then the parties can put on a stipulation with respect to finances and put on a trial with respect to custody and/or visitation, which action on their parts will significantly reduce their legal fees. It should be cautioned that some jurisdictions don't permit bifurcation but the vast majority of jurisdictions throughout this country do permit such a concept and it is certainly a cost savings device as it relates to a full trial on both monetary and custodial issues or a trial simply on monetary issues which often times can be much shorter and less expensive for the parties. This discussion cannot be completed without some further talk about legal fees. It is ethically mandated in most jurisdiction that lawyers and clients in virtually all matters except real estate closings enter into a retainer agreement which codifies the legal fee aspect of the case. That is true even in a prenuptial agreement. In most prenuptial agreement matters the lawyer is going to charge a retainer and an hourly rate or provides for a flat fee. In the case of a retainer and an hourly amount a retainer agreement is very important. One such retainer agreement which applies in large part to an actual divorce case is attached to this book as an appendix. Such a document can be easily modified as it relates to the terms of a prenuptial agreement and the lawyer's ultimate fees. It is mandatory in most jurisdictions from an ethical perspective that the parties' have separate retainer agreements with their own lawyers.

Chapter 3
Some of the Most Bizarre Topics Found In Prenuptial Agreements

Recently the Australian news in Adelaide tried to compile a list of bizarre or preposterous clauses found in prenuptial agreements, not only in Australia but throughout the world. The author will add to the list:

1. One client's prenuptial agreement limited her husband to watching one Sunday football game with friends. For a dedicated sports fan, such a choice could be tough. No word yet on whether or not the clause related to watching just the first half of the game or the second half or the entire game.

2. Another prenuptial agreement looked at the number of times sex is on the menu per week but lists all the different positions that must be tried.

3. Who gets the dog in the event of a breakup is fodder for many prenuptial and postnuptial clauses. Custody and visitation rights for pooches are almost as important as one's with respect to children. The one difference is that a prenuptial or postnuptial clause involving custody or visitation is against public policy whereas a clause relating to a pet is not against public policy.

4. One wife's prenuptial agreement limited her weight to 120lbs. The penalty for being over that weight is that she

gives up $100,000 of her separate property in the event that she weighs over 120lbs at the time that the prenuptial is sought to be enforced.

5. Another prenuptial agreement contains a requirement for random drug testing. Positive results can lead to fines, etc.

6. Another clause in a prenuptial stipulated precisely how long the husband had to work before he retired. He had to work until the age of 65.

Just because the above clauses exist doesn't mean they will be enforced by a court in your jurisdiction. Most of these bizarre clauses are obviously unenforceable but most prenuptial or postnuptial agreements are severable to the extent that if one of the clauses in the agreement is found to be unenforceable then the entire agreement is not deemed to be unenforceable.

It is clear based on the above clauses that couples should sit down well in advance of a marriage and make a list of concerns to be discussed and prepare a separate document unrelated to a prenuptial agreement stating each other's wishes and intentions. While this document certainly won't be binding, it can help clarify issues that are important in making the determination as to whether or not a prenuptial agreement is necessary and if so what causes or issues should be contained in such a prenuptial.

Chapter 4
What the Stats Say

Americans were interviewed and surveyed in 2002 by Harris Interactive with respect to how they view prenuptial agreements. At the time postnuptial agreements were very new and prenuptial agreements were starting to burgeon. The margin of era for the total sample was about 1.9%.

28% of all Americans surveyed said that prenuptial agreements make smart financial sense for anyone getting married. 25% of the public thinks that such agreements are for the rich and famous and not for regular people.

1 in 5 believes in true love and feels that prenuptial agreements are never needed when two people involved really love each other. Another 15% are totally convinced that a prenuptial agreement dooms a marriage right from the start. 12% found such contracts to be a good idea in general, but felt too uncomfortable to bring them up in their own relationship. Of those individuals the overwhelming majority were involved in a first marriage.

Men appear to be less comfortable than women with the subject of prenuptials. 10% of women say that a prenuptial is a good idea and 15% of men surveyed feel that bringing up the idea would make them feel uncomfortable. In reality, lawyers surveyed indicated that men overwhelmingly were the initial clients with respect to prenuptial agreements and that very few female clients appeared to initiate them.

Americans who live in households with children are significantly less likely than those without children by a 10% margin to believe that prenuptials make sense. This is probably attributable to the fact that prenuptials cannot legislate either visitation or custodial rights.

49% of divorced Americans believe that prenuptial agreements make financial sense under the right circumstances while just 1 in 5 married Americans feel the same way about their marriage. This makes sense because far more prenuptials are written for second marriages then first marriages.

45% of Americans see the biggest benefit of a prenuptial as allowing one to keep a fair share of the assets that he or she brought into the marriage or earned during the marriage. 1 in 5 Americans believes the prenuptial would make a divorce shorter, easier and less costly. Another 12% think of the children first. They see protection of the best interest of the children as the biggest benefit of a prenuptial agreement even though it is against public policy to legislate the best interest of a child in a prenuptial agreement.

15% of divorced Americans regret not having a prenuptial agreement because their spouse got too many of the assets they themselves earned during the marriage while another 7% regret the lack of a prenuptial since it would have made their divorce shorter and easier. The rationale behind this is most likely the fact that individuals, after a divorce feel "burned" by the system and never want to be exposed to the legal system again with respect to making decisions which will impact the future of their financial security.

Very few Americans at that time had prenuptial agreements. Even fewer had postnuptial agreement. Only 1% of Americans in

2002 had a prenuptial agreement. That number is much higher now even though it has not been quantified.

Fully two-thirds of Americans said that they did not want advice on prenuptials from celebrities given the fact that most celebrities who they had read about had negative results from trying to enforce their prenuptial agreements in court. Celebrities are a bad reference group for average people and there is recognition of that. They have three, four or even five marriages with outrageous demands. The McCartney case involving former Beatle Paul McCartney which was recently tried in England brought that more to the fore than perhaps any other case beforehand and that it got publicity not only in England but throughout the world.

Chapter 5
Living Together Agreements

It is impossible to have this discussion without first discussing finances and perhaps even having financial affidavit forms or financial worksheets completed. Those forms can be obtained from Attorneys or on line.

Each party should pull out their respective paperwork and share with their partner their current financial status which includes but is not limited to expectancies of immediate or future inheritances.

For parties who decide to live together, as opposed to marrying and hence not entering into a prenuptial agreement, a living together agreement which parallels much of the language which would be set forth in a prenuptial agreement has been recognized in many jurisdictions throughout the country as an enforceable contract in a civil court, as opposed to a matrimonial or family court. This would take more time to enforce, but would still have the indicia of validity.

Years ago, non marital cohabitation was rare due to the mores of society. Also at the time common law marriage was regulated in most states by marital laws.

Interestingly, family law certainly sanctioned business contracts and provided certain equitable relief for cohabitants in the 1950's and 1960's but no legal rights were created given the fact that courts viewed non-marital cohabitation as being socially undesirable.

All of that changed with the seminal <u>Marvin v. Marvin</u> California case in 1976, involving the famous actor Lee Marvin. That case on certain levels sanctioned cohabitation with respect to enforcement in court and provided financial relief under the right circumstances to a cohabitant.

Today, <u>Marvin</u> represents the dominant approach to cohabitation cases in at least 26 states and the District of Columbia. See Non-Marital Cohabitation: Social Revolution and Legal Revolution by Marsha Garrison in 42 Family Law Quarterly no 3 at p.315.

There have been a dearth of cases on a national level decided since <u>Marvin</u> and one of the key reasons is that many such cohabitation claims settle short of an appellate decision and hence don't appear as precedent in legal books.

Chapter 6
Religion and Prenuptials

Religious leaders are almost unanimous in their feeling that prenuptial agreements are favored with them. They feel that any potential document which can help save or preserve a marriage is worthwhile. They offer very little if any opinion about postnuptials because to a person they said that they had not been exposed to the topic in their practices.

There really is not a great deal of variance among religious leaders on this topic.

A reformed rabbi from Westport, Connecticut who was also trained as a lawyer, felt that there is very little guidance in Jewish theology with respect to the topic but did feel that after meeting with numerous congregants over the years that prenuptials had both helped to narrow the issues when there had been a divorce situation or permit a marriage to get off the ground that otherwise would not have gotten off the ground if one of the parties had not entered into the prenuptial agreement. She indicated that she had spoken to congregants about the issue of whether or not to actually enter into a prenuptial agreement when one of the parties balked at the notion and usually gave the advice that if the marriage is a non-starter because of the prenuptial then the parties should seriously consider entering into it and not view it with suspicion.

A Unitarian minister from Connecticut felt basically the same way. He had also counseled the members of his church community over the years with respect to the topic and had seen very few if any potential marriages fall apart as a result of the desire by one of the parties to enter into a prenuptial agreement. He recognized that from a financial perspective it sometimes makes sense to have such a document, especially when one of the parties has come into a small fortune from a family member and another family member feels that that sum should be protected in the possible case of a future divorce.

A Catholic priest had much less exposure to the topic. Divorce is clearly not favored in the Catholic church and remarriages after divorce without a church annulment prevents the party or parties from obtaining the sacraments of the church. The priest was educated to some extent about the issue and after a frank discussion agreed that in certain cases prenuptials did make a great deal of sense in that they had the strong possibility of saving or preserving a marriage that otherwise might have been in trouble.

As indicated previously, there is very little religious doctrine for many of the above religions on the topic.

In order to fully understand prenuptial agreements throughout the world one must draw attention to a wide spread institution future of marriage contracts enforceable under Muslim family law.

The Mehr or traditional Islamic brideprice, which functions as a prenuptial agreement in Bangledesh due to the default practice and which is only payable upon divorce. Mehr serves as a barrier to husbands from existing marriage, in which dowry can be divided into a standard price component in a term that ex anti compensates grooms for the cost of Mehr chosen by the couple. The contracts are well fair improving because they induce husbands to internalize the social costs of divorce for women.[1]

One nuance which has arisen in the Jewish religion relates to the concept of a "Get" and it's impact on prenuptial agreements.

Things get complicated in the Orthodox Jewish religion. Certain Orthodox rabbis require that prenuptial agreements be signed in advance of the marriage relating to the requirement that if one of the parties refuses to give a Get he or she will be liable for supporting the other party to the extent of approximately $150.00 per day for each day that the Get is not given.

The above clause cancels itself out if both of the parties are recalcitrant In California this support amount is deemed to be independent of civil obligations to pay support.

Other versions of Orthodox prenuptials provide that husbands will pay a liquidated damages sum of $150.00 or greater if the husband refuses to give a Get. Some rabbinic authorities say this agreement invites a coerced Get, which is invalid because husbands are required to give a Get willingly and without coercion. Thus, a liquidated damages provision forces him to give a Get under threat of monetary damages.

The most recent versions provide that if a husband refuses to give a Get after the parties have lived apart for approximately 15 months then it will be deemed as if he never intended to do so and the marriage is void *ab initio* and the marriage will be deemed annulled. In this case the children are still deemed to be legitimate because Jewish law does not recognize illegitimacy.

---

1 See Field, Erica "Muslim Family Law, Prenuptial Agreements and the Ermergenc of Dowry in Bangledesh"

There are a host of problems with various versions of these prenuptials which are set forth in the Appendix to this book. Suffice it to say that the provision does not work if the husband is too poor to pay the support.

The importance of a prenuptial agreement under Orthodox Jewish law transcends the actual document given the state of Jewish divorce law on family law litigation in this country.

Alexandra Leichter, an expert in family law from Beverly Hills, California has written a very learned argument on *the effect of Jewish divorce law on family law litigation. She notes that:*

> *"Jewish law requires that an Orthodox Jewish wedding be terminated not only by civil law, but also by a Jewish divorce, called a "Get". Without a Get the parties are not considered divorce and the consequences, especially for a woman are life-altering. . . . Until a woman obtains a Get from her husband, she is considered still married to her husband and has no ability to remarry or have children from another relationship. If she violates this law, she is considered an adulteress and all progeny of such a married woman from that subsequent relationship are considered Mamzerim which is loosely translated in the English language as illegitimate."*

Further, she notes that:

> *" A woman who cannot obtain a Get is considered an agunah-chained to her marriage."*

Even without a prenuptial at least one state has a Get law which enables a judge in a divorce case to award a larger proportionate interest in the marital property and/or increase in spousal support to the party whose spouse refuses to give her a Get.

Leichter notes that:

> *"This legislations is couched in terms of penalizing those who refuse to remove the impediments to the other party's ability to remarry. Although this statute is presently under constitutional attack in the courts, it has helped a number of women whose husbands would otherwise attempt extortion in exchange for the Get."*

Thus the import of the prenuptial agreement in Jewish orthodox law given the fact that rabbis have not been unmindful of this inequity and the potential for major extortion. In Israel, laws allow rabbis to order imprisonment, loss of driver's and professional licenses and other penalties to be imposed on the recalcitrant husband.

Hence, modern orthodox rabbis have devised as a remedy the drafting of a Jewish prenuptial agreement wherein the parties agree, as previously mentioned, prior to the marriage to give a Get. These prenuptial agreements further provide that the parties will submit the issue of the Get to the Beth Din (Jewish court of law) as an arbitrator. Leichter notes that "such arbitration clause should, theoretically, be enforceable by the civil court."

There is no published state court decision in this country where the enforceability of such prenuptial agreements has been tested by a married litigant.

Forms of these prenuptial agreements are set forth in the Appendix.

Reformed Jews don't have prenuptials as they relate to religious considerations because they don't believe that a Jewish divorce is necessary. They do not follow the rules of Jewish law. Conservative Jews don't need a prenuptial because their marriage contract has the Lieberman clause that essentially allows rabbis to free the woman in the event that she seeks a divorce.

It is clear from the above discussion, that the Jewish religion has far more "law" related to the topic of prenuptial agreements than any other recognized and organized religions.

Chapter 7
Prenuptial Agreements and their many Tax Consequences

It is essential that an individual entering into a prenuptial agreement or postnuptial agreement consult an attorney who is not only familiar with family law, but also with the tax consequences of transfers under family law. If the family law practitioner who is drawing up the prenuptial doesn't feel comfortable with respect to that issue then he or she should send the potential client also to a tax or estate planning lawyer or an accountant.

Many property transfers made pursuant to the terms of such an agreement involve tax consequences and from time to time the tax law does change and the agreement may need to be updated to reflect the changes in the tax law.

The guiding principle behind a prenuptial agreement is to transfer property or pay alimony in exchange for a release of marital rights. Hence the tax consequences will depend on when the transfer took place. If the transfer took place prior to the marriage then there could be gift tax results. Therefore the prenuptial agreement should stipulate that any transfer of property occur after the marriage. Obviously any postnuptial agreement will only involve property transferred after the marriage by definition.

The Internal Revenue Code provides that transfers between spouses and former spouses made incident to a divorce are tax free. Transfers within six years after divorce pursuant to the terms of a divorce decree are deemed to be incident to a divorce.

If the marriage ends in divorce, the prenuptial agreement will often times spell out property transfers and issues of alimony. Property transfers are not taxable but alimony, if spelled out clearly is taxable to the recipient and deductible by the payor.

To be deductible for tax purposes alimony payments must meet the criteria set forth in the Internal Revenue Code. They must be:

a)   made in cash;

b)   received by or on behalf of a spouse under a divorce or separation agreement;

c)   the payor's obligation to make the payments must end with the death of the payee;

d)   the agreement must not specifically designate that the payments are not alimony;

e)   the filing of a joint tax return is prohibited;

f)   the payor and payee's spouses must not be members of the same household at the time of the payments;

g)   payments cannot be fixed as child support; and

h)   the document cannot be orally amended between the parties.

One factor that the attorneys must consider is known as alimony recapture. If payments would otherwise qualify as alimony but decrease rapidly in the first three years following separation or divorce then they may be recharacterized as a property settlement by the Internal Revenue Service. Recapture does not apply to payments reduced due to death of either spouse. Alimony recapture if applicable occurs in the third year.

When a prenuptial agreement takes effect due to the death of a spouse the property is included in the decedent's gross estate and the recipient spouse must take the basis and the property equal to its fair market value.

In addition to using your prenuptial or postnuptial agreement to waive inheritance rights and state your particular intentions for passing on your property at death it's critical that you hire an attorney to prepare the correct estate planning documents which include but are not limited to a will, living trust, etc. that actually transfers your property as you intend at the time of your death.

It is essential that the estate planning mechanism suggested by an expert in the field mirror the terms set forth in the prenuptial agreement. If this is not done then the surviving party is often times forced to file a claim in the decedent's estate to enforce the prenuptial agreement. If the decedent's estate objects to the claim the surviving spouse and the decedent's estate which often means children from a first marriage can be involved in costly and protracted litigation.

In virtually every state there are laws that prevent one spouse from completely disinheriting the surviving spouse. These laws are generically referred to as the "statutory spousal elective share". It allows the spouse to renounce a will and claim a portion of the decedent's estate. A prenuptial agreement if found to be fair can waive the right under state law to claim a forced share this effectively causes one of the spouses to be disinherited.

One common mistake often made in prenuptials and postnuptials is that the party does not provide for death in the agreement and only contemplates and provides for divorce. In that scenario your spouse will automatically have the right to a spousal property election asking the court to give him or her an interest in the separate properties depending on who else in involved. For example if you had no children but your mother was still living at the time you passed away your wife would in most states be entitled to a one-half interest in your separate property estate and your mother would receive the other half.

Estate planning is critical for all couples planning on getting married or actually married. Successful estate planning transfers your assets to your beneficiaries quickly and with minimal tax consequences. It is not only for the wealthy.

The most common technique for estate planning is a will. Almost half of all people who die in the United States die without a will.

A will is a very basic document and in it should include the following elements:

1. Names of spouses, children and other beneficiaries;

2. Alternate beneficiaries in the event that a beneficiary dies before you;

3. Specific gifts such as an auto;

4. Establishments of trust if any;

5. Cancellation of debts owed to you;

6. Naming of an executor to manage your estate;

7. Naming of a guardian for any minor children;

8. Your signature; and

9. Witnesses' signatures.

Another issue that needs to be considered in estate planning and coordinated with a prenuptial or postnuptial is who will manage your estate if you cannot. This becomes important when someone becomes incapacitated either permanently or temporarily. The document that is used is called a power of attorney which allows one person to appoint someone else to act on his or her behalf.

Another technique which is widely in use and must be coordinated with a prenuptial or postnuptial agreement is a living will which is a kind of advance directive that comes into effect when a person is terminally ill. A living will allows you to specify the kind of treatment you want and specific situations.

It must be noted that estate planning is not a one time deal. There are a number of changes in your life that can call for a review or a complete change of your estate plan. The following are some of those changes, but are not meant to be comprehensive: the value of your estate changes significantly from the date of your last will, you marry or divorce, you have a child or a new grandchild, you move to a different state, the executor of your estate becomes incapacitated, one of your heirs dies or the laws affecting your estate plan change in your state. Lawyers specializing in this specialized area of the law should be consulted on a regular basis in this regard, in concert with the lawyer who drew up the prenuptial or postnuptial agreement.

Lawyers specializing in this specialized area of the law should be consulted on a regular basis in this regard, in concert with the lawyer who drew up the prenuptial or postnuptial agreement. It would also be a good idea to have the estate planning lawyer review the prenuptial or postnuptial agreement prior to its signing.

Chapter 8
The Pacelli Case and Legal Authority For Postnuptials

Mr. and Mrs. Pacelli married in 1975. At the time he was 44 and she was 20 and had just come to the United States from Italy. In 1985 Mr. Pacelli told his wife that he would file for a divorce against her unless she signed a postnuptial agreement which would give her $500,000 and half of their vacation home in the event of a divorce. Not long after he moved out of the house.

The parties had two children.

Mrs. Pacelli ultimately signed the agreement. Nine years later Mr. Pacelli brought a divorce action against Mrs. Pacelli in New Jersey. He was worth 11 million dollars at the time and had a large income. Mrs. Pacelli contested the validity of the postnuptial agreement.

The case was tried before the trial court which upheld the postnuptial agreement. The Appellate Court of New Jersey disagreed and said that the postnuptial agreement was not fair and that postnuptial agreements require closer scrutiny than prenuptial agreements. The court hung its hat on the fact that Mrs. Pacelli would have received much more money as a result of a divorce than she was getting in the postnuptial agreement. The court did not deny that she was represented by counsel, that he was represented by counsel, that there was full financial disclosure, that they were both of sound mind, etc. but still refused to enforce the postnuptial.

The court said that: we are persuaded that placing a mid-marriage agreement in the same category as a prenuptial agreement is inappropriate. . . the dynamics and pressures involved in an mid-marriage context are qualitatively different.

As this book is being written, the case of <u>David v. David</u> is being tried in the Superior Court at Hartford, Connecticut. It involves a postnuptial agreement and loads of money. Both sides made it clear that the case law throughout the country is thin with respect to postnuptial agreements and <u>Pacelli</u> is being cited by both as authority on both ends of the spectrum.

In <u>Crane v. Howard,</u> 1951 OK 282 the Oklahoma court ruled that a postnuptial agreement entered into between a husband and wife after their marriage was without effect and the right of either to take of the other's estate through succession by law. In other words a postnuptial agreement between a husband and wife not to dissent from the will of the other and waiving the right of the husband or wife to take from the other's estate under the law of intestate succession is not authorized by law in the State of Oklahoma and hence is invalid and unenforceable.

A seminal Massachusetts case of <u>Fogg v. Fogg,</u> 409 Mass 531 (1991), held that in a divorce proceeding the trial judge did not make a mistake in refusing to enforce an agreement made by the parties while they were married and not anticipating an immediate divorce. The alleged purpose of the agreement was to preserve the marriage but the evidence warranted the judge's findings that the agreement was not free from fraud because the wife despite her statements to the contrary was at the time only concerned with arranging a favorable financial settlement in the event of a divorce.

Few if any other cases throughout the country at least up until 2008 have had as much impact on the law of prenuptial agreements as Pacelli, Crane and Fogg.

Most postnuptial agreements are governed by basic contract law with the understanding that the terms can't be inconsistent with the public policy of the State in question.

Interestingly and quite recently in England following the case of Macleod v. Macleod, Dec. 17, 2008, the old rule which provided that postnuptial agreements were contrary to public policy has now been abolished. The decision of the Privy Council recognized that upholding postnuptial agreements may pave the way for couples to exert greater control over their assets in the future by agreeing during their marriage as to a fair outcome should they split up.

Chapter 9
Anecdotes

Tim and Jennifer were married in 1980. They each brought approximately $50,000 into the marriage. In the year 2000 Tim has assets in his name in the amount of 9 million dollars as a result of his interest in a hedge fund. Jennifer had assets in her name in the amount of approximately $700,000 which included a one-half interest in the parties' real estate.

Tim's partners in the hedge fund urged him to enter into a postnuptial agreement. He had no interest in the hedge fund prior to the marriage. The hedge fund managed assets of a value in excess of 100 million dollars. Tim had 3 partners in the hedge fund.

Jennifer agreed to enter into a postnuptial agreement. The postnuptial agreement called for her to get the entire house and $100,000 alimony for the first five years post divorce and then $75,000 per year alimony until Tim retired. Tim was 50 years old and Jennifer was 52 years old at the time they entered into the postnuptial agreement.

Approximately one year after the postnuptial agreement was entered into Tim entered into a relationship with his secretary and six months after that informed Jennifer that he wanted a divorce.

Jennifer hired an attorney and argued that Tim's conduct should disqualify him from upholding the validity of the postnuptial agreement.

The court disagreed claiming that the amount of money given to Jennifer was fair under the circumstances and that Tim's conduct arose well after the postnuptial agreement was entered into and was not in his contemplation at the time the postnuptial agreement was entered into.

Jennifer appealed to the Appellate and Supreme Courts of her state and both appeals were denied.   She was stuck with the decision of the trial court.

LESSON TO BE LEARNED: There is no guarantee that marital fault will automatically invalidate a prenuptial agreement.

We have previously alluded to "the talk" that should take place between people planning on getting married, married desiring a post-nuptial, or a living together agreement between same sex couples.

The talk obviously takes place in other contexts and is analogous to some of these situations.

A friend of mine is a huge college football fan. He is a fan of a certain school in the Midwest and his allegiance to that school is inviolate. He recently married and while there was no desire to put together a prenuptial agreement, there was a desire to have "the talk" long before any of the details of the wedding were even planned.

He approached the subject with his wife-to-be on a Sunday and they decided to go out to dinner in a public place the next Friday evening to have "the talk". Both parties were aware of the elements of it and "the talk" took place over a candlelight dinner at a local restaurant.

The football fan wanted to make it clear to his soon-to-be spouse that there were twelve weekends during the year starting in September and ending in January in which no plans were to be made with family, friends or other third parties. Those days, and most often Saturdays, were devoted to the football game either in person or on television. It was, from his perspective, a nonnegotiable item.

He told his future wife that on other weekends he would defer to her as it related to making plans but on these twelve fall weekends he wanted to be totally free to prepare for and watch the game in question and then talk on the internet with other similarly situated fans about the game.

"The talk" took place admittedly over a few glasses of wine and went fine. His future spouse thanked him very much for being totally frank about his plans and she had no objection to them.

She had relatives in California who she often went to see and he had absolutely no problems with her going to California on any weekend, including his football weekends even without him.

They were both mature, in their thirties and had dated extensively. The talk took place about six months in advance of the wedding and before any catering hall, band or flowers had been ordered. The talk worked perfectly and there is no reason why the talk, as it relates to a prenuptial or post-nuptial, can't have the same impact. That marriage is still going strong after more than 10 years. Unfortunately, his school, Notre Dame is not doing as well on the football team. There is apparently no relationship between the quality of the marriage and the quality of Notre Dame football.

LESSON TO BE LEARNED: Talk everything out before you enter into an agreement.

Carol and Jacob were married on October 26, 1991. At the time he had assets worth about one million dollars which included an interest in a retirement plan and she had assets worth about $300,000 which she received from her late grandfather's estate.

Five years after the marriage Jacob started an internet business and it really took off. By the year 2000 he was worth in excess of 10 million dollars and had 30 employees.

Carol did not work during the marriage as they had 3 children, one of whom had disabilities and was very difficult to raise at home but they insisted on doing it anyway.

In 2001 Jacob started a relationship with his secretary. Carol found out about the relationship in 2003 from e-mails and text messages on his phone. She confronted Jacob and he admitted the relationship and told her that he was in love with his secretary and that she was in the process of getting a divorce and that he planned on marrying her some day. Carol was shocked and stunned.

Carol brought an action for a divorce from Jacob not long after he admitted the relationship. At that time Jacob was worth about 15 million dollars, was earning $800,000 per year, had 3 very expensive cars one of which was a Porsche, had electronic equipment in the house worth over a million dollars and was really living the good life.

The family home was worth about 5 million dollars and was in both names.

In Carol's petition for a divorce she did not allege the existence of the prenuptial agreement. Jacob hired an attorney after he was served with papers and he alleged the existence of the prenuptial agreement and noted in his court documents that he intended to enforce the prenuptial agreement.

After extensive financial discovery a trial was scheduled in 2005. The trial lasted 3 days and the first order of business was the existence and validity of the prenuptial agreement. Carol put on 3 witnesses with respect to their financial circumstances at the time of the marriage and their financial circumstances at the time of the divorce. She also put on an expert medical witness about the condition of their son who is home bound and home schooled. The judge recessed the trial and wrote a lengthy seven page decision declaring the prenuptial agreement to be invalid on a number of grounds. He cited the fact that their financial circumstances had changed appreciably since the date of the marriage, the unanticipated circumstance regarding their son and the fact that Jacob was totally at fault for the breakdown of the marriage with respect to his relationship with his secretary.

The case was tried and Carol got half of the assets and $300,000 per year in alimony and child support until the youngest child attain the age of 18 and then $200,000 per year in alimony until her death, her remarriage, Jacob's death, or her cohabitation. She was also awarded $500,000 worth of life insurance to fund the alimony obligation.

LESSON TO BE LEARNED: Marital fault can sometimes invalidate a prenuptial agreement and a dramatic change in financial circumstances since entering into the prenuptial agreement almost automatically will invalidate the prenuptial agreement.

Eric is an advertising executive in New York City. His wife Donna is a stay at home mom in Stamford, Connecticut.

When they got married in 1990 they were in their early 30's, had very few assets and had no reason to enter into a prenuptial agreement.

Eric came up with an advertising campaign for a computer company and he won a national award for it. He was interviewed by a correspondent from Time Magazine and not long after the interview entered into a relationship with her. He had no intention of leaving his wife and four children for her and made it clear to her.

Eric's feelings started to develop more strongly for the correspondent and at or about the same time he got a $750,000 bonus from his advertising company and was made a full partner with equity in the company as a result of his efforts for the computer company.

Eric was very confused emotionally and told his wife that he wanted a postnuptial agreement. He told her that all the partners at the firm had one and even though their marriage was fine he and the firm would feel more comfortable if he had a postnuptial. Donna was very startled by Eric's request and said no to him. He prodded her for about a week and she conferred with her parents and continued to say no. Eric gave up on the idea.

She became very suspicious not long after the request for the postnuptial and started to notice that Eric was coming home on the train much later than usual. She hired a private investigator and the investigator caught him having dinner with the Time Magazine correspondent in New York. The private detective took pictures.

Donna confronted Eric with the pictures and he first denied that it was him and Donna showed him the report from the private detective and assured him that it was him. He then admitted to the relationship, including the length of the relationship and Donna filed for a divorce claiming marital fault on the part of Eric.

LESSON TO BE LEARNED: If the circumstances are suspicious at the time that you ask for a postnuptial you're probably better served not asking for it. There is an excellent chance that Eric and Donna never would have been divorced and the affair would have ended but for the repeated requests for the postnuptial.

John is 37 years old and is a plastic surgeon. He lives in Greenwich, Connecticut and earns $900,000 per year. He was married previously and paid alimony of $100,000 per year for a term of 5 years to his former wife. He had one child with her and also paid $50,000 per year in child support and was obligated to pay the cost of college for his child. It was a contentious divorce that took over 3 years.

Susan has never been married before and she is 31 years old. She has had three prior relationships but John is the first person with whom she has ever felt to be in love.

John and Susan live together for a year at his home before he popped the question and asked her to marry him. They set a wedding date of June 1, 2005. Susan was thrilled and told all of her friends both in Connecticut and California, where she grew up. Her entire family living in California, Colorado, North Dakota, Louisiana and Connecticut planned to come to the wedding. 300 people were invited to the wedding and John was going to pay for the wedding in full.

Approximately one month before the wedding John told Susan that he needed to have a prenuptial agreement. He told her that he really didn't want to have one but that his accountant told him that he had to have one in light of his contentious prior divorce and his obligations to his daughter both contractually and in his Will.

Susan was caught completely off guard and really didn't know what a prenuptial was. She contacted a lawyer friend and got some basic understanding. Approximately 2 weeks later and 2 weeks before the wedding John provided Susan with a prenuptial agreement which called for her to get $1,000 per month alimony for the number of months of the marriage and a flat sum of $50,000 if they got divorced. John told her that he couldn't make any provision for her in his Will because he was leaving everything to his daughter. He did tell her that if he and Susan had children he would leave any child or children with his relationship with Susan the same amount that he was leaving to Alice, the child from his first marriage.

Susan was befuddled and hurt. Another week later John gave her a financial statement showing that he had over 3 million dollars of assets exclusive of the residence in Greenwich which was in his name. Susan had approximately $150,000 in assets which she had saved for the past 8 years in her capacity as a nurse. John had told Susan that she didn't have to work during the marriage.

Susan went to see a lawyer and the lawyer informed her that the prenuptial agreement was unfair. As she left the lawyer's office she cried and was unclear as to what she should do.

She confronted John that night and the discussion was very contentious. He told her that he was not going to negotiate the terms of the prenuptial and if she tried either directly or through her attorney to change any of the terms he would call off the wedding. She was now more than hurt. She was mad. What should she do?

Susan talked to family, friends and her attorney and made the decision that she needed to get more alimony if they were married for more than 5 years and a piece of his estate if he predeceased her and they were still married. She didn't want to deal with him directly so she instructed her lawyer to contact his lawyer. Her lawyer made that call. His lawyer contacted him and he categorically turned down her request. The 7 days leading up to the marriage were horrible but he finally relented on the Thursday before the Saturday wedding and agreed to give her what she was looking for. She had an awful taste in her mouth and that ruined, to a large extent her wedding day. It also set their marriage off on a rocky start.

LESSON TO BE LEARNED: The prenuptial agreement was proposed way too late in the game. However, there is law in certain jurisdictions that an agreement could be enforced even though it was signed on the day of the wedding. It is impossible to predict what will be deemed to be sufficient time, but a good rule of thumb is to execute the agreement well in advance of the actual marriage. There is one case which actually says that a prenuptial agreement discussed before the marriage and signed after the marriage was valid, but no appellate court in this country has ruled on that issue.

Phil and Doreen were married for 10 years. It is a second marriage for both of them. Phil's wife died approximately 14 years previously and Doreen was divorced, receiving alimony but no child support. Both parties were in their 50's and Doreen's children were in college.

After the engagement and before the marriage Phil inherited a parcel of land on which a motel stood. The parcel of land was valued in the vicinity of $900,000. The matter had yet to go through probate and Phil didn't even think about it as he and Doreen were planning their wedding which was going to be a gala fest with over 200 guests.

About a week before the wedding Phil was at a cocktail party and met a matrimonial lawyer. He told him about the wedding and the inheritance and the matrimonial lawyer suggested to him that he have a prenuptial agreement. Phil had never thought about a prenuptial agreement and approached Doreen that evening. She was upset and hurt and said that it wasn't necessary because this marriage was going to be forever.

Phil thought about this for most of the week and Friday, the day before the wedding he contacted the matrimonial lawyer. The lawyer suggested that he and Doreen come in that afternoon. Doreen was quite busy and her mind was certainly distracted but she agreed to come in and meet.

They spent about 3 hours at the lawyer's office and drew up an agreement which insulated the $900,000 from Doreen and gave her approximately $100,000 if there ever was a divorce between the parties.

Doreen was never advised by the matrimonial lawyer that she had a right to seek independent counsel. Phil's schedule of assets attached to the agreement was fairly comprehensive but Doreen's was only about 3 sentences, recounting the fact that she had a pension from her prior employment as a teacher and virtually nothing else. It didn't even mention the alimony that she was receiving and about to lose as a result of the marriage.

The document was signed in the lawyer's office and in the document it said that Phil was represented by that particular matrimonial lawyer and that Doreen chose to represent herself. Doreen barely read the agreement before she signed it.

The marriage lasted about 10 years and really fell apart because one of Doreen's children died and it put so much stress on the marriage that Doreen simply could not continue on with Phil.

Her husband was quite upset, hurt and angry when he was served with divorce papers. He remember that there was a prenuptial agreement and put a call into the matrimonial lawyer. The matrimonial lawyer had passed away. Phil hired a divorce lawyer to represent him in defending the divorce action. He brought the prenuptial agreement to the divorce lawyer and the divorce lawyer said that it was probably not enforceable. He cited the fact that Doreen did not have independent counsel, the Agreement was not fair at the time it was sought to be enforced because by then Phil was worth over three million dollars which included the land and Doreen was worth approximately $500,000. Phil said that he still wanted to try to enforce the Agreement and the parties went before a retired judge for a pretrial.

The judge spent about 5 minutes with the Agreement and told everyone present, including both clients that the Agreement was unenforceable. He recommended that Doreen receive $200,000 plus $2,000 a month alimony for a term of approximately 5 years. That total package added up to approximately $320,000 and after taxes approximately $290,000 in Doreen's pocket. Phil's legal fees for the proceedings were about $30,000. Phil certainly suffered a financial loss as a result of the retired judge convincing everyone that the prenuptial was invalid.

What are the lessons to be learned from this proceeding. First, a prenuptial as previously stated should not be raised a week before a wedding. Second, both parties need independent representation and if one of the parties agrees to waive independent representation then it must be a clear waiver and not simply a statement hidden in the middle of an agreement. Third, an attorney should never be giving legal advice to an unrepresented party, especially with respect to a prenuptial which is being entered a day before the wedding.

The retired judge was correct and the result was sound at least in the mind of an appellate court.

LESSONS TO BE LEARNED: The lessons be learned are legion and should be recognized by all matrimonial lawyers preparing prenuptial agreements and by all clients entering into prenuptial agreements.

Chapter 10
Prenuptials and Athletes

The author had an opportunity to spend a week or so at the US Tennis Open in 2007 and spoke to a number of athletes, agents, and news people about the concept of prenuptials or post nuptials and athletes.

Tennis players at the top of their games earn upwards of $5 million a year in prize money and $15 million a year in endorsements. Some earn even more. They travel around the world as the tennis season is based in Australia in January, in the Paris region in May, the London area in July, and in New York in September. Oftentimes many of them have live-in boyfriends or girlfriends who travel with them. Players at the lower level oftentimes use these individuals as their schedulers and they perform invaluable tasks for the tennis players so that the tennis players can concentrate more on their games rather than laundry, restaurant reservation, etc.

I spoke with a top ten player in the world on the male side and he indicated to me that he has no live-in girlfriend but that when he does get married he will definitely have a prenuptial agreement. He was incredulous about the fact that most players have never even contemplated the situation. He said that the subject does come up among players and they say that they are too busy to even think about hiring a lawyer and putting together such a document.

One agent of a major player said that while he recognizes that he has a fiduciary duty to his client he also recognizes that he has a duty to the live-in girlfriend and he didn't want to antagonize his relationship with the player by bringing up a prenuptial agreement. He felt that word would immediately get to the girlfriend and, in his words: if you lose the girlfriend as an ally you will ultimately lose the player as your client.

Many players have girlfriends at home but, due to their celebrity status, have relationships on the road and some have even become fathers as a result of these relationships without their girlfriends even knowing. They obviously have no agreement with the mother of the child and they are often found paying exorbitant amounts in child support just to avoid the publicity or having their girlfriend find our about the situation. This happened with a famous player from France.

So What To Do?

It is certainly suggested that agents make their clients aware of the situation in a way that doesn't antagonize the girlfriend or boyfriend, if the player involved is a female. It should be spun in such a way so that the agreement would be mutually beneficial to both the player and the girlfriend. It should be noted in this regard: to the girlfriend, either directly or through the player, that without such an agreement, and most specifically, a live-in together agreement, she could end up with nothing, which is certainly not a desirable situation for her.

Another situation which arises in this regard is in what jurisdiction to put together the agreement. The answer to that is a very simple one. The agent or lawyer employed must research the laws of the specific state in this country or country outside the United States to see where it would be most beneficial to enter into the agreement. The agreement will oftentimes have a choice of law provision which will set forth which laws of which jurisdiction apply to the agreement.

Since players at this high level often have multiple residences, the choice of law provision becomes one more of economics than of actual physical residence. In other words, the player restless has to decide in conjunction with his or her advisors which laws make more sense for the enforceability of the agreement and other such variables related to the agreement.

This chapter is obviously not unique to tennis players, but also applies to athletes in other sports and entertainers throughout the country. The only thing that sets tennis players apart from some other athletes is that they not only travel throughout the United States but they often travel throughout the world to play in events and in view of this, the contributions made by the live-in girlfriend or boyfriend are often greater than in other sports and a possible choice of law provision becomes far more relevant to them in negotiating a prenuptial agreement. This is something that their lawyer or agent should raise with them almost immediately when the topic comes up. The agent issue raises an interesting question. Many agents are not attorneys but still have a fiduciary duty or relationship with the athletes whom they represent. They need to be schooled in the issues of prenuptials and not cowed by their clients, at least to the extent of knowing who to refer their client to in various jurisdictions not only throughout the country but throughout the world.

Chapter II
Prenuptial Agreements: the Evolutionary Process in Connecticut

Since the author practices law in Connecticut and has a handle on Connecticut law as it relates to prenuptials and postnuptials, it was felt that a discussion of prenuptials from an evolutionary process should be had utilizing Connecticut law. After much confusion about the validity or invalidity of prenuptial agreements, a Connecticut Court in the case of McHugh v. McHugh, 181 Conn. 482 (1980), set forth the principles guiding the validity or invalidity of prenuptial agreements in Connecticut.

The Connecticut Supreme Court required that the agreements: (1) formed up a contract validly entered into; (2) its terms did not violate statute or public policy; and (3) the circumstances of the parties at the time the marriage is dissolved are not so beyond the contemplation of the parties at the time contract was entered into as to cause its enforcement to work injustice.

McHugh remained the law of the state of Connecticut for over fifteen years and numerous cases followed and distinguished McHugh in Connecticut. A case said that agreements entered into on the eve of a marriage were suspect. Many practitioners interpret this to mean a forty-eight hour role. More specifically, any agreement entered into within forty-eight hours of the marriage was, by definition, suspect.

Other cases recognized that both parties must have independent legal representation. Importantly in this regard they must have chosen their own lawyers instead of having a straw lawyer sit in at the behest of the other party. It was the favored process in these cases that each party pay their own lawyer and that both lawyers be involved in the draftsmanship of the agreement as well as signing off on the agreement. This led to the proliferation of CYA letters in which a lawyer who felt that the agreement was unfair would send a letter to the client informing the client of that, even though the client decided to sign the agreement against the lawyer's advice.

On or about1994, there were so many cases distinguishing McHugh, that the Connecticut State Legislature upon the urging of the Family Law Committee of the Connecticut Bar Association of which the author is a member started to debate the Premarital Agreement Act, which has been enacted in many jurisdictions throughout the country. The Act is an Appendix to this book.

The stated purpose of the purposed legislation was to recognize the legitimacy of premarital agreements in Connecticut and not to constrain such contracts to a rigid format so as to limit their applicability. In other words, the Act was to be far more liberal in interpreting premarital agreements than prior law.

More specifically, the Act established standard in guidelines for premarital agreements. It includes provisions with respect to what agreements may have in them, what they can include and also under what conditions the agreements will be enforceable.

The Act specifically provides that a premarital agreement may not have any provisions which adversely affect a child of the marriage.

Further, in Section 5 it provides that an agreement can be modified in writing after the marriage so, in essence, it is like a will.

It is an executory contract that can be modified at any time by the parties without consideration.

Even with the existence of the Act, certain cases in Connecticut after 1995 have still found prenuptial agreements to be invalid. Some of the reasons are as follows:

1. One of the parties did not have any financial disclosure prior to the meeting in the offices of the attorneys when the agreement was executed.

2. The agreement did not attach written financial disclosures.

3. The agreement was executed as a result of endue influence and lack of free will.

4. The agreement was not signed by one of the parties.

5. The agreement was not delivered by one of the parties after signature of the other party.

The state of the law in Connecticut and in jurisdictions throughout the country is still in flux. Cases come out on a daily or weekly basis which uphold or invalidate prenuptials, largely dependent on the facts of the case. There are hard and fast rules but they are very factually intensive and cannot be analyzed in a vacuum without knowing the particular facts of the case at hand.

Chapter 12
Litigating the Premarital Agreement

Why would there be litigation if there is a prenuptial agreement in place? The answer to this question is not so simple, however, since (unfortunately) nearly every agreement in any situation (whether it is a commercial transaction or a premarital contract) can be questioned, challenged and contested. In my effort to make sense of this seemingly confusing subject, I thought it would be useful to focus on two major topics. First, it should be helpful to present an overview of the essential aspects of a typical lawsuit. Secondly, based on the Uniform Premarital Agreement Act which has been adopted in many American states, we will then discuss some of the essential legal issues that could become the subject of litigation regarding the Premarital Agreement at the time of a divorce.

There are a variety of options available and they are all strategic.

It must be remembered that in all jurisdictions in this country except for Texas divorce cases are tried to a judge and not a jury so much of the strategy involved would relate to the understanding of whom the judge might be and what the judge's prior history is with respect to upholding or disallowing prenuptial or postnuptial agreements. It is easy for a lawyer to research prior cases decided by a particular judge if you are afforded the luxury in advance of knowing who the judge on the case will be.

In most courts there are 3 or 4 possible judges who may sit on a case and it is not known until the actual day of trial who the judge will be.

A call to a friendly clerk a day or two in advance of trial could solve the conundrum and provide you with the name of the judge and hence afford you the opportunity to do research on the judge's prior decisions.

The next bit of strategy relates to whether or not the prenuptial agreement should be argued in advance of the divorce trial in the form of a motion in limine or whether or not it should be argued part in parcel of the divorce case.

The answer to the above question may relate to whether or not issues of fault which would come out at a divorce trial but not necessarily in a motion in limine would effect the judge either directly or subliminally in a way that would make it harder or easier to uphold the prenuptial agreement. The more practical route if there is no egregious fault is to put the issue of the prenuptial before the judge at the very start of trial by way of a motion in limine and argue the issue. This will not only decide the issue at bar in advance of trial but will potentially save your client thousands and thousands of dollars in legal fees.

OVERVIEW: THE ESSENTIAL ASPECTS OF A LAWSUIT

The Pleadings and The Issues

The "pleadings" are the legal papers that are used to start the lawsuit and to define clearly the disputed issues for the judicial authority in your State (usually the Judge) to decide. Pleadings are particularly important in lawsuits (or "cases") involving Premarital Agreements. For that reason, it is worth saying a few words about how to "plead" the Premarital Agreement; that is, how to shape and define the legal issues related to Premarital Agreements in the pleadings.

The Plaintiff's Complaint is the initial pleading. The law requires the Complaint to state in specific, numbered paragraphs (known as "allegations") every fact essential to that case. Divorce laws and the legal procedures in divorce cases tend to differ from State to State. Generally, however, all Complaints should allege the essential facts upon which relief may be granted and all Complaints should make a "claim for relief." The "relief" sought is ultimate Judgment the Plaintiff is seeking. In divorce cases, the relief sought is a Judgment of Dissolution of Marriage (i.e. a divorce Judgment) and Court Orders such as: alimony, distribution of property, child custody and child support, etc. In divorce cases where the parties did not have a Premarital Agreement, the Plaintiff's Complaint will list all of these claims for relief plus "any other relief" available under your State's divorce laws.

Importantly, if the parties have entered into a Premarital Agreement, the party seeking to enforce that Premarital Agreement must introduce that fact into the lawsuit. Otherwise, if neither party has introduced the Premarital Agreement into the case, the Court will not consider that Agreement. And the Court Orders for alimony, distribution of assets, liabilities and all other financial Orders will be based on the State's general statutes governing all divorce cases. Some states follow "community property" laws. Others follow the law of "equitable distribution." If either party wants the Divorce Judgment to deviate from the general laws of community property or equitable distribution, and enter Court Orders consistent with a Premarital Agreement, it is that party's responsibility to make sure that the Premarital Agreement is introduced into the case. Usually, this is accomplished initially through the pleadings.

Once the Premarital Agreement is introduced into the case, the relief (i.e. the Court Orders) may include the specific relief provided to the parties in that Agreement as long at the Premarital Agreement is found to be legally "valid" and enforceable. Before we get to the issue of the "validity" of Premarital Agreements and the law of contracts, a few additional comments about the essentials of every lawsuit.

How To Respond When Served With A Divorce Complaint

After the Defendant receives service of the Complaint, the Defendant must first decide whether to submit to the jurisdiction (the power) of the Court in the particular judicial area that the Plaintiff has chosen. While there are some instances where a Defendant might have a strategic reason for attempting to have the case heard in a different State, those strategic considerations are beyond the scope of this Chapter. Assuming there is no other State or other Court that could or should decide this case, the Defendant must "Appear" in the case in order to be an active participant in the litigation. Usually, the Plaintiff and the Defendant "appear" through their attorneys who file a form known as an "Appearance." A party who chooses not to hire an attorney should file a "pro se" appearance. Any Defendant who fails to "appear" in any case either through an attorney or by way of a pro se appearance is playing with fire. It goes without saying that avoidance or denial is the worst possible response to a lawsuit because the Court may render a judgment of default against a non-appearing Defendant who has been properly served with the Complaint.

The initial pleading that the Defendant files in response to the Plaintiff's Complaint is the "Answer." The law requires that the Answer must be limited and the responses to the Plaintiff's Complaint must be specific. The Defendant must either admit or deny each fact stated or "alleged" in every paragraph of the Complaint. Sometimes a Defendant will answer that s/he has "insufficient knowledge upon which to admit or deny" a particular allegation in the Complaint. That response is not considered an alternative to an admission or denial. It is a denial.

Every lawyer learns that the function of the pleadings is to frame the issues. Once a party introduces the Premarital Agreement into the case and the other party files pleadings in response, the pleadings are then considered to be "closed" and the issues to be litigated and decided in that case have been clearly framed and defined.

It is worth repeating. If you have a Premarital Agreement and you want the case to be decided in accordance with that Agreement, it is your responsibility to introduce that Agreement into the case. Otherwise, your Premarital Agreement will not be considered and the case will be decided according to the general laws of community property or equitable distribution that govern all divorce cases in your jurisdiction.

Types of Issues: Issues of Fact and Issues of Law

In a typical lawsuit, there are two main types of issues: (1) issues of fact and (2) issues of law. When a party to the litigation admits an allegation stated in the other party's pleadings, that statement is then considered a true "fact" and no further evidence is needed to "prove" the existence of that fact. When a party denies an allegation stated in the other party's pleadings, each issue has been framed and is ready to be decided at the trial.

Issues of law are also known as the "ultimate" issues. Whenever a premarital agreement is raised in either party's pleadings, the essential issues for the court to decide are: (I) Whether the Premarital Agreement was properly formed as a matter of law. (2) Whether the Premarital Agreement should be enforced as a matter of law. At the risk of confusing you, I note that sometimes a court can only decide these "ultimate" issues by reference to the facts of a particular case. In those instances, the court sometimes will blur the distinction between types of issues with terms like "mixed issues" of law and fact. To clearly understand the essential aspects of every trial, it is important not to blur this distinction. Therefore, we will consider all issues to be either issues of fact or issues of law.

Evidence vs. Fact

Before turning to the fundamental questions or issues involved in the trial of a Premarital Agreement case, it is also worth mentioning the difference between the definition of a "fact" and the legal meaning of "evidence." Only after the distinction between "evidence" and "fact" is clarified, we will then be able to address clearly the issues of fact and law that are presented in the trial of a Premarital Agreement case.

To illustrate the difference between "evidence" and "a fact," consider first the difference between general "information" and "evidence." For example, the book that you are holding in your hand right now is not "evidence." Nor is it considered a "fact" from a legal point of view. The information on these pages is simply "information." If you were to ask a judge to accept this book as "evidence," you would first "proffer" this book as evidence during a hearing or a trial. This book would be marked as an Exhibit so the "record" would correctly "identify" it as potential evidence. Once a bit of information is offered and identified as evidence, the court must then decide or "rule" whether that evidence is "admissible" based on the law of evidence. Only after a court rules that proffered evidence is admissible is it then possible for that evidence to be considered as a possible "fact." Any evidence that is not admissible cannot even be considered as a possible "fact." Obviously, a Premarital Agreement must be admissible as evidence before it might be considered as a "fact" in any case. We will return to this question in the next section of this Chapter.

"Fact Finding:" Court Trials vs. Jury Trials

It is very rare that a divorce case is presented to a jury for a jury trial. Nevertheless whether the case is tried to a court or a jury, it is crucial to understand clearly the extremely important function of "fact finding" that occurs during any trial.

The fact-finding process in all cases is the process whereby the "finder of facts" decides whether one or the other party's evidence is "true." This involves deciding which evidence to *believe*. A party's sworn testimony, once it is found to be admissible (and, as discussed above, then transformed from "information" into "evidence") is not yet transformed into a "fact." All evidence only becomes transformed into "fact" after the judge "finds" (or "believes") that evidence to be *true*. For example, one party might claim that he or she did not know the divorce case would be decided according to the Premarital Agreement. In that case, if the Premarital Agreement has been introduced into evidence and if it contains language stating that the parties acknowledge and agree that the divorce will be decided in accordance with that Agreement, the judge will most likely "find" that the party's testimony is not "credible" or believable if that party signed that Premarital Agreement. If the judge "finds" that the signed Premarital Agreement speaks for itself on this point, that party's testimony will be rejected as untrue regardless of how adamant that party may be. This example of the "fact finding" role of the court in litigated cases is crucial to the entire process of judgment.

During a trial, the judge is routinely called upon to choose between the sworn testimony of two or more witnesses who flatly contradict each other. The judge must decide whether to believe one witness's "story" or the other's story (since two flatly contradictory statements cannot both be true.) Obviously, every witness takes an oath and is sworn to tell the truth, the whole truth, and nothing but the truth. Yet, when those witnesses testify in direct contradiction to each other, the court's job is decide which party is telling *the [one and only] truth*. This is an awesome power and responsibility known as "finding the facts." When the judge *finds* that the testimony of one party is more believable, and thus true, the judge has concluded (or "found") that one party is more "credible" than any other party on that point. Once the evidence (either sworn testimony or a document) is found to be credible and, therefore true, is it *found* to be a *fact*. Any evidence that is not believed is rejected and that evidence is not transformed to the legal status of "fact." Although all of the other evidence in the case (including all of the testimony of the witnesses and all of the documents admitted into evidence during the trial) retains its legal status as "evidence," NONE of that evidence is "fact" unless the judge "finds" it to be fact.

To most clients and parties involved in litigation, this difference between "evidence" and "fact" is foreign. It is strange. Unusual. Most people simply don't understand or realize clearly the scope and extent of the power our law gives to the "fact finder." Also, most people don't fully realize how absolutely essential it is for a judge to "find" the facts. We naturally assume that we are truthful. We all consider ourselves to be honest. Yet, whether you are a saint or a scholar, if your statements (your testimony in court) are not believed to be true for any reason, then your statements are not transformed into "fact."

Most people don't truly fathom the depth of the importance of this essential judicial function known as "fact finding." Because this is a central foundation upon which our entire legal process depends, it bears repeating. Only the evidence that the court "finds" to be true is true; and only that evidence the court finds to be true is transformed from "evidence" to "fact. And, moving on to the next step in the process of decision, the law provides that only after the facts have been found, can the court then proceed to the next level in the process of judgment, namely, to reach the ultimate legal conclusions necessary to "decide" the case. Why? Because all legal "conclusions" in every case must be based solely upon on the facts. Therefore, logic dictates that only after the process of fact finding may the court then proceed to reach the ultimate conclusions and decisions upon which to render "judgment" ending the case.

With these essential aspects of a lawsuit clearly in mind, we can next turn to the specific kinds of issues that arise in cases involving litigation of Premarital Agreements.

THE TRIAL OF A PREMARITAL AGREEMENT CASE

Burden of Proof

As noted above, in every Premarital Agreement case, there are at least two broad questions. (1) Whether the contract was validly formed and (2) Whether the contract should be enforced. In every trial of a Premarital Agreement case, each of the parties has a different burden of proof. The party who is seeking to introduce the contract and to enforce the contract has the burden initially to prove that it was formed in accordance with the requirements of the law. This is known as proving the validity of formation of the contract. After that party has met this burden of proof, the party "against whom enforcement is sought" then has the burden to prove that it should not be enforced. In other words, the party defending against the Premarital Agreement has the burden to prove that it is legally invalid. In this Chapter, we will refer to the party who is seeking to avoid the Premarital Agreement as the "defending party."

Validity of Formation

The Uniform Premarital Agreements Act, which has been adopted in many states, provides very simple and straightforward requirements for the formation of a Premarital Agreement. According to that Uniform Act as adopted in many states, as long as a Premarital Agreement is: (1) in writing and (2) signed by both parties, it will be enforceable without "consideration." This is a statutory definition that is very different from the definition of how a contract is normally or typically formed. Any first year law student will tell you that a contract is not valid without "consideration." Yet, the statutory test for determining whether a Premarital Agreement was properly formed bypasses all of the nuances of traditional contract law related to "consideration" and, instead, the Uniform Premarital Agreements Act provides that the marriage serves as consideration for the Premarital contract.

Thus, the statutory test to determine the validity of the formation of a premarital agreement is very simple and uncomplicated. Because it is only necessary as a matter of law for a Premarital Agreement to be "in writing" and "signed," then a Premarital Agreement could be validly formed if it were written on the back of a napkin and both parties signed that napkin. (Mention Stephen Spielberg/Amy Irving case?) If it is so easy to create a Premarital Agreement, what is all the fuss about when a party seeks to enforce that Agreement? That is the next subject and it is the essential question to be decided in the trial of every Premarital Agreement case.

Should the Premarital Contract Be Enforced?

Once it is determined that the Premarital Agreement is in writing and signed by both parties and it is admitted into evidence the burden of proof shifts to the party defending against the enforcement of that contract. Because the issues related to "enforcement" are the most central issues in every premarital agreement case, the remainder of this Chapter will focus on the legal questions that the party defending against the enforcement of a Premarital Agreement must prove.

According to the terms and provisions of Uniform Premarital Agreement Act, the party "against whom enforcement is sought" may prove any one or more of the following to invalidate that Premarital Agreement.

1) Such party did not execute the agreement voluntarily; OR

2) The agreement was unconscionable when it was executed or when enforcement is sought; OR

3) Before execution of the agreement, such party was not provided a fair and reasonable disclosure of the amount, character and value of property, financial obligations and income of the other party; Or

4) Such party was not afforded a reasonable opportunity to consult with independent counsel.

Because each of these alone is sufficient to invalidate the Premarital Agreement, it is likely that a lawyer who is planning to challenge a Premarital Agreement will seek to discover whatever information as may exist regarding each of these criteria. Accordingly, each of these points will be addressed separately.

(1) *Voluntary execution of the agreement*

Regarding the question whether a party signed an agreement "voluntarily," one of the most important factors is the time when that agreement was signed. A related question is whether that party was under duress when the contract was negotiated and signed. A party who was presented with an agreement to sign on "the eve of the wedding" may be able to demonstrate that the agreement was not "voluntarily" signed. Although this "timing" factor might relate more directly to the issue of duress, the courts have considered the timing of the signing in relation to the date of the wedding in relation to the question whether that party's signature was voluntary. Obviously, because of this factor it is prudent to take steps to avoid the claim at trial that the proximity in time between the wedding and the hasty, pressured signing on the "eve" of the wedding requires the court to find that the party did not sign the agreement voluntarily.

In addition to the evidence of the timing of the signing, other sources of proof of whether a party signed "voluntarily" will normally include testimony from any witnesses who were present at the time when the Agreement was signed. Two of the witnesses are the lawyers who drafted that Premarital Agreement. Therefore, whenever a party claims that a Premarital Agreement was signed under duress or the signature was not voluntary, the other party will invariably call as a witness the lawyer who represented the party making that claim. It is common sense that a lawyer would never allow his or her client to sign an agreement knowing the signature was involuntary. It is also a matter of professional responsibility or, worse, potential professional negligence for a lawyer to allow his or her client to sign against the client's will. Thus, the testimony of the lawyer would be important to prove that basic fact.

(2) *Agreement unconscionable when signed or when enforcement is sought*

What does the word "unconscionable" mean? According to Black's Law Dictionary, an "unconscionable" contract is defined as one "that no promisor with any sense, and not under delusion, would make, and that no honest and fair promisee would accept." Black's Law Dictionary (8th Ed. 2004). There are many cases in which courts have added further to this definition. For example, courts in many states have defined an unconscionable agreement as "one which no man in his senses, not under delusion, would make, on the one hand, and which no fair and honest man would accept, on the other."

Although some questions are "mixed questions" of law and fact, the Premarital Agreement Act specifies that in every case the question of "unconscionability" is a question of law for the court to decide. Thus, in every case the judge must decide whether any aspect of the Premarital Agreement or whether the Agreement as a whole "shocks the conscience." This is not simply a test whether an agreement is "fair." An agreement may be unfair but still enforceable because it is not "unconscionable."

Returning to the requirements of Uniform Premarital Agreement Act, the Court must first examine the facts and circumstances as of the date when the agreement was made. Only after the Court is persuaded that the facts and circumstances surrounding the negotiation and signing of the Agreement "shock the conscience," may the Court then conclude that the Agreement is invalid as a matter of law.

If there is no finding that the facts and circumstances in existence at the time when the Premarital Agreement was made were unconscionable, the Court will then decide whether it would be unconscionable to enforce the Premarital Agreement as of the date of the trial, i.e. the date when one party is seeking to enforce that Agreement. To put this issue in perspective, we should simply assume that any party who is defending against a Premarital Agreement will assert that the Agreement is "unfair." Nevertheless, as pointed out above, the term "unconscionable" extends far beyond the reach of simple "fairness." An unfair agreement will be enforced. Only an unconscionable agreement will be invalidated.

While it is beyond the scope of this Chapter to speculate regarding terms in a Premarital Agreement that might be unconscionable, one illustration will demonstrate the point. Let's assume that the Premarital Agreement clearly states that the defending spouse will not receive any alimony in the event of a divorce. Assume also that the parties were married for a long time—more than twenty years. Let's add the assumption that the defending party is suffering from a debilitating illness that did not exist when the agreement was negotiated and signed. Finally, assume that the party seeking to enforce the agreement has extraordinary wealth, the unfettered ability to pay alimony, and suppose the Premarital Agreement did not provide for any sharing of the wealthy party's assets. In this case, we could easily see how a judge could conclude that it is unconscionable to deprive the defending party of any alimony solely because that party once promised not to seek any alimony and that promise was in the form of a valid waiver of any claim to alimony. We may assume that most courts in such a case would reach the conclusion that the Premarital Agreement is invalid because this result shocks the conscience.

(3) Before execution of the agreement, the defending party was not provided a fair and reasonable disclosure of the amount, character and value of property, financial obligations and income of the other party.

The usual practice in negotiation and drafting Premarital Agreements is to attach a Financial Disclosure Statement to the Agreement when it is signed. Doing this certainly shows the Court at a later date the nature of that financial disclosure. The only issue then is whether that financial disclosure was "reasonable."

The reasonableness of a party's financial disclosure is not necessarily the same as determining whether the party committed a fraud by falsely disclosing or failing to disclose each aspect of his or her financial condition. The question of fraud is a much stricter test. The question whether a party's disclosure was "reasonable" involves determining if a reasonable person in possession of that financial information would have sufficient basis upon which to engage in the negotiation of that Premarital Agreement.

A party defending against enforcement of a Premarital Agreement might claim that he or she never saw that financial information. Alternatively, that party might claim that he or she did not understand the financial information that was produced prior the signing of the Premarital Agreement. Ironically, it is sometimes actually true that the party in receipt of the financial disclosure did not see that financial information because it is frequently exchanged between the lawyers representing the parties in the negotiation and drafting of the agreement.

Does it mean the Premarital Agreement will automatically be invalidated simply because the defending party's lawyer did not show the financial information to the client? Put another way, if the client never sought to ask his or her lawyer to see that financial information should the Court invalidate the entire Premarital Agreement even though the other party provided fair, reasonable and ample financial disclosure? The law's answer to this question is not simple. But it is logical. The answer some Courts have given to these questions is that the knowledge of the lawyer is *imputed* to the client. That is, those Courts have decided that any financial disclosure provided to the lawyer was provided to the client. Those Courts have applied the law of "agency" by which the client is the principal and the lawyer is the agent. As the agent for the client, the knowledge of the lawyer is the same as the knowledge of the client.

This rule makes sense logically and as a matter of common sense and simple fairness. Any other rule would be oppressive and grossly unfair since it is impossible for a party to do more than to give the financial disclosure. It is not the responsibility of one party to insure that the other party reads the financial documents that have been provided.

(4) The defending party was not afforded a reasonable opportunity to consult with independent counsel.

While it may be obvious that each party should have separate legal representation at the time when the Premarital Agreement was negotiated and signed, it is not normal or usual or even natural for every person about to marry to seek out a lawyer. After all, two people who are about to marry are not in an adversarial position. If they were, they certainly wouldn't be considering marriage!

Because many parties contemplating marriage might be inclined to engage the same lawyer, the legal problem this causes is that the one lawyer with whom the parties consulted may be found to be less than "independent." Thus, if two clients go to one lawyer to draft a Premarital Agreement, that agreement could later be found to be legally invalid because of the appearance of a lack of "independent" representation. That Agreement will definitely be invalidated if the defending party did not have at least the opportunity to consult with independent counsel.

It is not necessary that the defending party actually consulted with independent counsel. The law only requires that each party have the *opportunity* to consult with independent counsel. If a party chose not to consult with a lawyer before signing a contract, that is certainly acceptable. But, for purposes of this Chapter, we are assuming that the defending party is now claiming that there was no *opportunity* to engage or consult with a lawyer at the time when the agreement was negotiated and signed. In order to avoid this problem, the Agreement should clearly state that each party was afforded the full opportunity to consult with independent counsel.

In conclusion, because each of the statutory criteria is separated by the word " "OR" this means that any one of the above criteria, if proven, may well lead to the court concluding that the Premarital Agreement should not be enforced.

Interpretation of Contracts

The final subject to discuss involves the law regarding interpretation of contracts. Once it is proven that the contract was formed according to the law and after it is determined that the contract should be enforced, it remains for the court to determine if all of the terms and provisions (also known as the "remedies") are clear and unambiguous. This discussion turns to basic rules and laws pertaining to the interpretation (or "construction") of contracts.

The general rule is that whenever a court is asked to enforce a contract, the court must determine if the language of the agreement is clear an unambiguous. Where the language of the contract is clear and unambiguous, the contract is to be given effect according to its terms. A court will not "torture" words to create ambiguity where the ordinary meaning leaves no room for ambiguity. Any ambiguity in a contract must emanate from the language used in the contract rather than from one party's subjective perception of the terms.

As we have already discussed, the party defending against enforcement of a Premarital Agreement is, by definition, dissatisfied with the terms of that agreement. It is likely that the defending party will argue that some aspect of that agreement is "ambiguous." Because this is the position that the defending party will take at trial, it is important to take steps to draft the language of a Premarital Agreement carefully and precisely. Nevertheless, even with the utmost care and precision, it is possible that the English language will fail in the task of clearly and unambiguously expressing the intent of the two parties. If that occurs, the Court might be required to interpret, or construe, the terms and provisions of the Premarital Agreement.

Assuming the Court is required to construe the contract's terms, the party seeking to enforce the contract, at least, is not faced with the drastic remedy of a court refusing totally to enforce the entire agreement.

Related to the subject of contract interpretation is the question whether a term or provision of the contract is invalid because it is against public policy. While our legislatures, not our courts are responsible for determining the public policy of our states, our courts are nevertheless asked on occasion to find that a contract term should not be enforced because enforcement would be contrary to public policy. Although the subject of public policy is beyond the scope of this Chapter, there are aspects of some Premarital Agreements that are particularly dubious.

Provisions That Should Be Disregarded Based On Pubic Policy

Some parties negotiating Premarital Agreements might insist that the other party must promise to have sexual intercourse at least four times a week. Others might insist that a party must promise not to gain more than ten pounds over a specific weight. Provisions of this nature are offensive to any reasonable notion of "public policy" and should not be enforced.

Because the statutes have made it is so easy to create a Premarital Agreement, our legislative public policy seems designed to encourage Premarital Agreements. One policy reason for encouraging parties to enter into Premarital Agreements is to avoid the difficult, expensive, and often traumatic process of divorce litigation that burdens the courts in every state. Nevertheless, while Premarital Agreements may be encouraged, insufficient attention has been given to the types of provisions that are offensive to a reasonable and enlightened sense of public policy. If lawyers and parties negotiating Premarital Agreements become tangled in the web of disputes over such absurdities as the amount of weight a spouse may gain or the number of times a couple must have sexual relations, the institution of marriage will suffer.

Whenever possible, in order to encourage parties to marry and to discourage lawyers and parties from seeking ridiculous provisions in a Premarital Agreement that could cause the fragile pre-marital relationship to crumble, and, last but not least, in an effort to encourage parties to avoid senseless litigation in the event of a divorce, Courts and legislatures should draw clear lines on the basis of sensible public policies between provisions in Premarital Agreements that are appropriately tailored to the fair and reasonable resolution of the genuine issues in marital dissolution cases and those "issues" that are based on ludicrous demands that have no place in a premarital contract.

Chapter 13
A Change In The Law

Most states throughout the country as previously discussed, have adopted Premarital Agreement Act. Prior to the adoption of the Act courts were governed by what is known as the common law. That is the case law which evolved prior to the enactment of the statute.

The common law focused largely on whether the Agreement complied with ordinary principles of contract law. Such issues as separate representation, financial disclosure and unconscionability were analyzed. Under the common law and on many occasions if a court found that a marriage had broken down because of the fault of one of the parties the prenuptial agreement may not be enforced. Similarly where the economic status of the parties changed dramatically between the date of the entry of the Agreement and the date of dissolution then the Agreement was found to work an injustice and was not enforced.

In the 1990's most state legislatures passed the Premarital Agreement Act which applies to all premarital agreements entered into after the date of adoption of the Act. The key elements under the Act are:

1. That the parties executed the Agreement voluntarily.

2. That the Agreement was fair when it was executed and fair when it was sought to be enforced.

3. Before the execution of the Agreement each party provided a fair disclosure of their finances.

4. That each party was afforded a reasonable opportunity to consult with independent counsel of their choosing.

The Act indicates that parties to a premarital agreement may contract from many things including but not limited to:

1. The rights and obligations of each of the parties.

2. The right to buy, sell, use, transfer, exchange, abandon, lease, consume, mortgage, dispose of or otherwise manage and control property.

3. The disposition of property upon death.

4. The modification or elimination of spousal support.

5. The making of a will.

6. The ownership rights in a life insurance policy.

7. The right of either party as a participant under a retirement plan.

8. The choice of law governing the construction of the agreement which means the law of which state would apply.

9. Any other matter of their choosing.

Both the common law and the Act obviously speak to the issue of financial disclosure and the topic is one of the key issues in litigation which arises from a prenuptial agreement. We have attached in the appendix a financial affidavit.

Simply stated the requirement of fair and reasonable disclosure may be satisfied if each party in advances of the signing of the

Agreement executes a signed and sworn financial affidavit showing income, assets, liabilities and expenses. Each party must also be given a reasonable opportunity to receive confirming documentation such as bank statements, etc.

In representing parties the practitioner must make sure that all assets, liabilities and income is disclosed. To often just assets and perhaps liabilities are disclosed alone without the disclosure of income. Parties should not rely solely on income tax returns since they do not reflect non-taxable income.

While the disclosure must be full and frank it need not necessarily be detailed to the penny. It is recommended that each spouse disclose not only their annual gross income but their interest if any in family trusts and potential inheritances. This helps defend against a challenge by either party that he or she did not disclose the value or extent of the financial rights which were waived.

It should also be considered with respect to financial disclosure that legal documents such as wills, trusts or pension plans may conflict with the premarital agreement and could lead to costly litigation down the road. It is absolutely essential that all beneficiaries are appropriately designated and that a will is prepared to show the intent of the party.

If there is a question as to the value of an asset value unknown should not be shown on the disclosure document. That could lead to problems in the future. The better course of conduct would be to hire an appraiser or a forensic accountant to come up with evaluation of something like a closely held business. This may cost some money early on but will avoid costly litigation down the road.

Chapter 14
Celebrity Prenuptial Agreements

There are very few celebrity marriages, especially second celebrity marriages that don't include a prenuptial agreement.

Everyone knows about details regarding Donald Trump, Paul McCartney and Barry Bonds. Actually the Bonds' story was mentioned earlier in this book.

Some of the most bizarre clauses in prenuptial agreements can be found in celebrity prenuptials.

Without discussing the identities of the parties celebrity prenuptial agreements have included the following clauses. There are no guaranty that these clauses are enforceable. One celebrity husband limited the wife's weight to 120lbs or less and in the event that she weighs more at the time of the divorce she must relinquish $100,000 of her separate property.

Another prenuptial required a celebrity spouse to provide random drug tests with financial penalties set forth in the prenuptial agreement.

Yet another required a celebrity husband to pay $10,000 each time he is rude to his non-celebrity wife's parents. What does rude mean? Who knows it wasn't defined.

Celebrity divorce attorney Robert Nachschin has said that "everything is legal unless you are dealing with custody of children or child support."

"People have their own little peculiar peccadilloes that they are concerned about" said celebrity attorney Leon F. Bennett, who once represented Marlon Brandon.

Many high profile prenuptials and postnuptials contain confidentiality clauses that keep them out of the public eye. Those confidentiality clauses may not be enforceable in the event that the prenuptial is litigated in court.

Infidelity clauses are common. Michael Douglas has reportedly agreed to pay Catherine Zeta-Jones millions should he stray from her and Denise Richards made similar requirements of husband Charlie Sheen.

With respect to celebrities "the problem is implied distrust" said Jeremy Ritzlan a long time Los Angeles marriage and family therapist. There is good reason why celebrities, especially high wealth celebrities need to have a prenuptial agreement or a postnuptial agreement no matter how unromantic the concept.

One doesn't need to look much further than Paul Macartney and Heather Mills. The former Beatle is believed to be worth around one billion dollars and ended up forking up over around 200 million dollars to his ex-spouse who claimed that he had abused her.

Neil Diamond was divorced from Marcia Murphy after 25 years of marriage and paid her somewhere in the vicinity of 150 million dollars. They had no prenuptial agreement.

When Steven Spielberg and Amy Irving divorced in 1989 the pair did have a prenuptial agreement but Irving contested it claiming that she lacked legal representation when it was signed. Before the issue was resolved Spielberg ended up paying her around 100 million dollars.

Harrison Ford paid ex-wife Melissa Mathison 85 million dollars and a piece of future earnings after 17 years of marriage and the claim that he was having a relationship with Calista Flockhart. They had no prenuptial agreement and it is posited that if Ford had an Agreement his payment would have been substantially lowered.

The same can be said for Kevin Costner and Cindy Silva. She claimed that he has having extra marital affairs and he reportedly paid her as much as 80 million dollars in 2004 without the benefit of a prenuptial. She was his childhood sweetheart.

Michael and Diandra Douglas did not have a prenuptial when they split in 1997 after 22 years of marriage. He is believed to have paid her 45 million dollars, one-third of his fortune.

There are many more examples, some sordid and some normal which have involved celebrities and prenuptials and postnuptials over the years and it is impossible to chronicle all of them in a book of this nature.

Chapter 15
The Future

Will prenuptial agreements continue to dominate in the future? Will postnuptials become the wave of the future? Will living together agreements be more prevalent?

In a recent poll of The American Academy of Matrimonial Lawyers, 49% of these divorce attorneys cited an increase in post nuptial agreements during the past 5 years. Interestingly enough, 58% of the respondents most frequently draw up the agreements as a result of a request made by both parties.

Married couples, whose numbers have been declining for decades have finally slipped into a minority of the population according to an analysis of new census figures by the New York Times.

The American Community Survey found that 49.7% or 55.2 million of the nation's 111.1 million households in 2005 were made up of married couples, just shy of the majority and down for more than 52% five years earlier.

Marriage clearly has been facing more competition. A growing number of adults are spending more of their lives single, or living unmarried with partners. (New York Times To be Married Means to be Outnumbered Oct. 15, 2006).

Andrew A. Beveridge, a demographer at Queens College is quoted in the article as saying "It's partially fueled by women in the work force; they don't necessarily have to marry to be economically secure."

The Yale Daily News did a study on January 24, 2007 and came up with the conclusion that fewer college couples plan on marrying post graduation.

A study in the State of Washington which was chronicled in Seattle PI.com on May 11, 2007 noted that the number of couples who live together without marrying has increased tenfold since 1960, the marriage rate has dropped by nearly 30% in the last 25 years and Americans are waiting about 5 years longer to marry than they did in 1970.

USA Today concluded that young adults are definitely delaying or deferring marriage. Among men ages 20-29, 73% said that they had never been married in 2006 compared with 64% in 2000.

There are a number of good reasons to consider a living together agreement. It will certainly help to protect your finances by clarifying financial commitments. It is more than sensible when only one of you owns the home that you both intend to share and allows you to look ahead to put into place contingency plans for events such as children, long-term illness or death.

Living together agreements are not enforceable in many states but are enforceable in other states as binding contracts.

With respect to the above there is a common myth that if two people are living together for a certain amount of time then it is tantamount to what is known as a common law marriage. This is a myth. A good example is if the rules and laws of intestacy do not apply where a couple is not married and when and if the relationship ends, the unmarried couple does not have the benefit of being able to apply for pension sharing orders which are available to married couples who are divorcing.

At its core a cohabitation agreement details the division of property and possibly a monetary settlement if one of the parties moves out. This protects both parties from petty disagreements.

So what does the above mean for the agreements which are chronicled in this book? Probably that living together agreements are more the wave of the future than any other document.

Many states in this country have approved domestic partnership or civil union statutes. Only Massachusetts, California and Connecticut currently permit marriage between same sex couples.

There has recently been a proliferation of prenuptial, postnuptial and living together agreements among individuals of the same sex who have entered into a domestic partnership or a civil union. The reason is simple. By virtue of the existence of a domestic partnership or civil union many rights including but not limited to the following attach to the relationship:

1. Rights to make medical decisions effecting the other party.

2. The right to act as a conservator for a domestic partner who is unable to make financial decisions.

3. Inheritance - the right to inherent a share of the partner's property even if there is no will or the surviving domestic partner is cut out of the will in its entirety.

4. Right to paid leave - a domestic partner has the right up to six weeks of paid leave in some states to care for a domestic partner or a child adopted by the domestic partnership.

5. Health insurance - some states require insurance companies to provide spouses with insurance coverage to offer the same coverage for the partner of a domestic partner and their children.

As a result of the above many domestic partners have entered into prenuptial agreements and some have actually entered into postnuptial agreements.

No reported decisions have been located nationally dealing with the validity or invalidity of such Agreements but there is no reason to believe that any such Agreement would be any more or less valid or invalid for a domestic partner as opposed to a Husband or Wife in a more traditional marriage. The law is currently burgeoning in this area and expect there to be a body of law within the next five years or so which deals with the topic. Domestic partners also, expect more states to have approved marriages between same sex couples within the next five years. At least one additional state has already done such as this book is being written.

Living together agreements more so than prenuptial or postnuptial agreements also indicate the property that each party has brought into the relationship. If the couple later decides to marry, the living together agreement will not be valid and should be replaced if necessary by a premarital agreement.

It is predicted that the future will be bright for all of these agreements and as the law continues to evolve with respect to individuals living together and same sex marriages, then even more of these agreements will become prevalent.

Post-script

In April, 2011, the Connecticut Supreme Court, in the case of Bedrick v. Bedrick, a case of first impression in Connecticut, decided that postnuptial agreements are valid and enforceable.

According to the court:

> "Because of the nature of the marital relationship, the spouses to a postnuptial agreement may not be as cautious in contracting with one another as they would be with prospective spouses and they are certainly less cautious than they would be with an ordinary contracting party. With less caution comes greater potential for one spouse to take advantage of the other. This leads us to conclude that postnuptial agreements require stricter scrutiny than prenuptial agreements. In applying special scrutiny, a court may enforce a postnuptial agreement only if it complies with applicable contract principles and the terms of the agreement are both fair and equitable at the time of execution and not unconscionable at the time of dissolution."

The court then defined what constitutes a fair and equitable postnuptial agreement:

> "The terms of a postnuptial agreement are fair and equitable at the time of execution if the agreement is made voluntarily and without any undue influence, fraud, coercion, duress or similar defect. Moreover, each spouse must be given full, fair and reasonable disclosure the

amount, character and value of property, both jointly and separately held… this mandatory disclosure requirement is the result of a deeply, personal marital relationship."

The court also directed how a court in the future should determine the validity of a postnuptial agreement:

"In determining whether a particular postnuptial agreement is fair and equitable at the time of execution, a court should consider the totality of the circumstances surrounding execution."

It is clear from the above, that at least the Connecticut Supreme Court and perhaps other courts throughout the country when they consider the issue in the future have determined that a postnuptial agreement deserves and requires stricter scrutiny than a prenuptial agreement fir the reasons set forth above.

It also appears clear after discussions with attorneys who represent gay and lesbian couples, that postnuptial agreements are as common among gay and lesbian couples as they are among straight couples and obviously in Connecticut they also should take heed of the recent edict from the Connecticut Supreme Court.

Conclusion

It is clear that prenuptial agreements are still burgeoning throughout the country. Postnuptial agreements have just started to take hold and more and more matrimonial lawyers are writing them for clients in marriages with problems. This is especially true given the fact that the economy is quite difficult and more couples are content to stay together with the knowledge that they have financial protections in the form of a postnuptial agreement.

Living together agreements, given the fact that more and more couples are living together for an extended period of time before marriage are becoming more prevalent.

With the advent of same sex marriages there is clearly another group of people who can take advantage of the benefits of one or more of these documents. It is certainly predicted that in the future more than two states will approve same sex marriage. There should be some healthy debates in the 2008 presidential campaign and thereafter regarding this topic.

About the Author

Mr. Kent is a practicing attorney and principal in the law firm of Meyers, Breiner & Kent in Fairfield, Connecticut. He has been practicing law for 33 years and has been included in *"Best Lawyers in America"* since 2004. He is a former past Chair of the Bridgeport Bar Association Family Law Section.

Mr. Kent has also authored "Fighting for your Children: A Father's Guide to Custody" and "Solomon's Choice" along with a number of sports books.

He has been a contributor to MSNBC on the topic of divorce law.

APPENDIX A

APPENDIX

THIS AGREEMENT entered into this   day of , 200_,
by and between   , of   ,

          , (hereinafter referred to as the "Husband-to-be") and ,
of   ,   , (hereinafter referred to as the "Wife-to-be");

WITNESSETH:

WHEREAS, the parties intend to be married within a short
time; and

WHEREAS, both the Husband-to-be and Wife-to-be have
been married previously and have children by his and her former
marriage; and

WHEREAS, the Husband-to-be has an estate consisting of
property as more specifically set forth in Schedule "A" annexed
hereto, which is an approximate statement of the assets, liabilities
and income of the Husband-to-be; and

WHEREAS, the Wife-to-be has an estate consisting of
property as more specifically set forth in Schedule "B" annexed
hereto, which is an approximate statement of the assets, liabilities
and income of the Wife-to-be; and

WHEREAS, each party acknowledges that full and adequate
disclosure of the property, estate, income and expectancies of the

other party has been made to the complete understanding and satisfaction of each party; and

WHEREAS, neither party has requested information which has not been provided; and

WHEREAS, each party has been fully advised and informed by counsel representing each of them as to their respective rights, and each has had advice of independent counsel of his or her own choosing, which counsel has fully explained the legal effect of this Agreement; and

WHEREAS, except as otherwise expressly set forth herein, each of the parties desires to keep all of her or his property, now owned or hereafter acquired before the marriage, free from any claims that the other party might otherwise acquire by reason of the marriage or by one party surviving the other; and

WHEREAS, each party is desirous of, and this Agreement has the purpose of, settling, surrendering, waiving, relinquishing, releasing, discharging and barring, and each party is willing to and intends to finally settle, surrender, waive, relinquish, release, discharge and bar, any and all claims, rights, interests or the like either presently or hereafter has or may have also and against the other arising as a result of any marriage to the other against the income, assets, property, estate or the like of the other, whether such income, assets, property, estate or the like, is now and/or hereafter obtained or acquired, including, but not limited to, any and all claims, rights, interests and/or the like to alimony, support, separate maintenance, assets, property, estate, assignment of property, pension rights, dower, curtesy, life insurance, widow's allowance, rights to elect against the Last Will and Testament of the other (whether now or hereafter executed), elective shares, distributive interests, allowances of any and all kinds accruing to a surviving spouse in and to the estate of a deceased spouse by virtue of Federal laws, laws of the State of _____ or any other state or jurisdiction, now or hereafter in force, intestacy, or the like, all except as hereinafter expressly provided; and

WHEREAS, each of the parties is relying, expressly and to a substantial extent, upon all provisions of this Agreement and the honoring of all of said provisions and, as a result of such reliance, will take certain action and will fail to take certain other action, which has extremely significant and important personal, financial and other effects on each of the parties, including, but not limited to, the following:

a) The parties may enter into a marriage ceremony with each other and may marry the other, which marriage neither party would enter into but for all provisions of this Agreement and the expectation that both parties shall at all times hereafter fully and faithfully perform and be bound by all provisions of this Agreement, and the further expectation that both parties shall at all times hereafter be absolutely and forever precluded and estopped from seeking to receive or receiving any benefits or imposing any obligations on the other which are or may be greater than or different from those expressly provided for in this Agreement.

b) The parties shall perform all provisions of this Agreement.

NOW, THEREFORE, in consideration of the forthcoming marriage and in further consideration of the mutual promises, covenants, provisions, undertakings and releases hereinafter set forth, and for other good and valuable consideration, the sufficiency of which is hereby acknowledged by the parties, the

Husband-to-be and the Wife-to-be hereby mutually and reciprocally agree as follows:

I. The parties declare that notwithstanding the fact that this Agreement is being entered into shortly before the contemplated marriage, it is not a sudden act.

Each party represents and acknowledges that he and she, respectively, have had separate, independent, and competent legal representation by an attorney of his and her own respective choice, and that each party hereto has reviewed and counselled with his or her own such respective attorney for a substantial period of time, all in connection with all legal and equitable rights of each in and to alimony, support, separate maintenance or similar benefits and in and to the income, assets, property, estate or the like, of the other as a result of any such anticipated marriage, all matters regarding this Agreement and the legal and practical effect of all provisions of this Agreement, all from the inception of negotiations in connection with this Agreement, privatehttp://autos.aol.com/?adl=18089ly and in the absence of the other party. Each party further represents and acknowledges that he and she, respectively, has a full and complete understanding of all of his or her said rights in and to said alimony, support, separate maintenance, similar benefits, income, assets, property, estate and/or the like, all matters regarding this Agreement, and the legal and practical effect of all the provisions of this Agreement. Each party further represents and acknowledges that:

(a) he and she does hereby freely and voluntarily enter into this Agreement; and

(b) that each party is entering into this Agreement with full knowledge of its terms and conditions; and

(c) that neither party intends to contest the validity of this Agreement in whole or in part, and that this Agreement is fair and equitable and not entered into as a result of any fraud, duress, coercion, or the like.

2. The Husband-to-be's estate, consisting of any property, real, personal, and mixed, of whatever kind or nature and wheresoever situate, heretofore or hereafter acquired by him up until the day of the marriage, whether titled in his sole name or in joint name with any person or persons other than the Wife-to-be (hereinafter referred to as his "separate property") shall remain and be his sole and separate property, subject entirely to his individual control, use and enjoyment, the same as if he were unmarried; and the Wife-to-be shall not acquire by reason of the contemplated marriage, for herself, her heirs, assigns or creditors, any interest in the Husband-to-be's separate property or estate or right to the control thereof, or any interest in the income, appreciation, increase, rents, profits, dividends, or property acquired by reinvestment, arising from his separate property (hereinafter referred to as "increase in his separate property").

The Wife-to-be hereby agrees in consideration of the contemplated marriage that she will and does hereby waive, release and relinquish unto the Husband-to-be all right to the use and control of his separate property and the increase and appreciation in his separate property and that she is absolutely precluded and estopped from making a claim against his separate property and the increase and appreciation to his separate property or modifying the terms of this paragraph irrespective of any circumstances hereafter existing or changes in circumstances hereafter occurring. She further agrees that the Husband-to-be shall have the right at all times to dispose of any part or all of his separate property and the increase and appreciation in his separate property, including retirement plan benefits that are not paid out during his lifetime, by deed, will or otherwise, on his sole signature, hereby ratifying and consenting on her part to any and all such disposition of his separate property and the increase and appreciation in his separate property or estate.

3. The Wife-to-be's estate, consisting of any property, real, personal, and mixed, of whatever kind or nature and wheresoever situate, heretofore or hereafter acquired by her up until the day of the marriage, whether titled in her sole name or in joint name with any person or persons other than the Husband-to-be (hereinafter referred to as her "separate property") shall remain and be her sole and separate property, subject entirely to her individual control, use and enjoyment, the same as if she were unmarried; and the Husband-to-be shall not acquire by force of the contemplated marriage, for himself, his heirs, assigns or creditors, any interest in her separate property or estate or right to the control thereof, or any interest in the income, increase, appreciation, rents, profits, dividends, or property acquired by reinvestment, arising from her separate property (hereinafter referred to as "increase in her separate property").

The Husband-to-be hereby agrees in consideration of the contemplated marriage that he will and does hereby waive, release and relinquish unto the Wife-to-be all right to the use and control of her separate property and the increase and appreciation in her separate property; and that he is absolutely precluded and estopped from making a claim against her separate property and the increase and appreciation to her separate property or modifying the terms of this Paragraph irrespective of any circumstances hereinafter existing or changes in circumstances hereinafter occurring. He further agrees that the Wife-to-be shall have the right at all times to dispose of any part or all of her separate property and the increase and appreciation in her separate property, including retirement plan benefits that are not paid out during her lifetime, by deed, will or otherwise, on her sole signature, hereby ratifying and consenting on his part to any and all such disposition of her said separate property and the increase and appreciation in her separate property or estate.

4. In the event legal title to any particular asset, property, estate and/or the like, and/or any and all such increments, additions, appreciation and/or the like thereto and/or income therefrom, is in the name of both the Husband-to-be and the Wife-to-be at the time the parties cease living together after any such marriage to the other, same shall be either divided or sold forthwith after any such ceasing living together, upon reasonable terms, and the net proceeds of any such sale, if applicable, shall be divided evenly by the parties, except that either party in any such division shall first be given credit for his or her contribution to such with pre-marriage assets or dollars.

5. The Husband-to-be and the Wife-to-be mutually and forever renounce, release, waive and relinquish all claims which each may have in or to any property or estate hereafter received by the other party from a person not a party to this Agreement, by gift, bequest, devise, or inheritance. Said property shall be considered and treated in the same manner as separate property in the preceding paragraphs.

6. The Wife-to-be hereby further waives and releases any and all rights and claims of every kind, nature and description that she may acquire as the Husband-to-be's surviving spouse in his estate upon his death, including (but not by way of limitation) any and all rights of intestacy, any and all rights of election to take against the assets passing under the Husband-to-be's Last Will and Testament, any rights or claims for a widow's allowance, any trust created by him, or any other augmented basis for determining the statutory share of a surviving spouse under any statute now or hereafter in force and effect in any jurisdiction and any and all rights or claims of homestead or dower in and to the real property of the Husband-to-be now owned or hereafter given to, devised to, or inherited by him, and any rights or claims for a widow's allowance during the administration of the Husband-to-be's estate.

7. The Husband-to-be hereby further waives and releases any and all rights and claims of every kind, nature and description that he may acquire as the Wife-to-be's surviving spouse in her estate upon her death, including (but not by way of limitation) any and all rights of intestacy, any and all rights of election to take against the assets passing under the Wife-to-be's Last Will and Testament, any rights or claims for a widower's allowance, any trust created by her, or any other augmented basis for determining the statutory share of a surviving spouse under any statute now or hereafter in force and effect in any jurisdiction and any and all rights or claims of homestead or curtesy in and to the real property of the Wife-to-be now owned or hereafter given to, devised to, or inherited by her, and any rights or claims for a widower's allowance during the administration of the Wife-to-be's estate.

8. Notwithstanding anything to the contrary provided in Paragraphs _____ and _____ of this Agreement, any jointly owned property of the parties with rights of survivorship to the surviving party shall become the sole property of the surviving spouse with the surviving spouse to have full use, enjoyment and the right to dispose of said property as he or she deems appropriate.

9. Nothing contained herein shall preclude the Husband-to-be from giving, devising, or bequeathing to the Wife-to-be through a Last Will and Testament or other testamentary substitute any property which he may choose, in which case the terms of such Last Will and Testament or other testamentary substitute shall be controlling and shall supersede the terms of this Agreement in the event of the Husband-to-be's death. This provision shall not be construed as a promise or a representation that any such gift, devise or bequest will be made by the Husband-to-be, and the making thereof or other provisions for the Wife-to-be shall not be construed to operate as any abrogation or termination of this Agreement or as any waiver of any other of the rights of either party.

10. Nothing contained herein shall preclude the Wife-to-be from giving, devising, or bequeathing to the Husband-to-be through a Last Will and Testament or other testamentary substitute any additional property which she may choose, in which case the terms of such Last Will and Testament or other testamentary substitute shall be controlling and shall supersede the terms of this Agreement in the event of the Wife-to-be's death. This provision shall not be construed as a promise or a representation that any such gift, devise, or bequest will be made by the Wife-to-be, and

the making thereof or other provisions for the Husband-to-be shall not be construed to operate as any abrogation or termination of this Agreement or as any waiver of any other of the rights of either party.

II. The parties, by reason of their affection for each other, and otherwise, sincerely desire that any such marriage to the other is successful and that they will live with each other the rest of their natural lives. In order to encourage any such marriage and to promote marital tranquility and serenity between the parties after any such marriage while the parties are living together, and an amicable resolution of certain issues in the event the parties cease living together after any such marriage, they agree, in the event the parties' marriage is annulled or a decree of dissolution, divorce or legal separation is entered by any court of competent jurisdiction or an action has been commenced seeking an annulment, dissolution, divorce or legal separation, as follows:

a. Neither party shall at any time pay periodic (temporary or permanent) or lump sum alimony to the other, and each party knowingly and intentionally waives the right to claim or receive alimony from the other at any time, now or in the future.

b. Except as provided in Paragraph 4 above, neither party shall receive as a division of assets the other party's separate property or increases and appreciation to the separate property.

c. Neither party shall at any time pay any portion of the other party's counsel fees, and each party knowingly and intentionally waives the right or claim to receive counsel fees from the other at any time, now or in the future.

12. a.   So long as it is lawful to do so, the Husband-to-be agrees to execute any consent form required under federal gift tax law to treat all gifts made by the Wife-to-be to her children, or any person who may be hereafter born to or legally adopted by any one or more of the Wife-to-be's children, as having been made one-half by each of them, so long as such election does not require the use of any part of the Husband-to-be's federal unified transfer tax credit.

b.   So long as it is lawful to do so, the Wife-to-be agrees to execute any consent form required under federal gift tax law to treat all gifts made by the Husband-to-be to any one or more of his children, or any person who may be hereafter born to or legally adopted by any one or more of the Husband-to-be's children, as having been made one-half by each of them, so long as such election does not require the use of any part of the Wife-to-be's federal unified transfer tax credit.

13.   Each of the parties agrees that in case the other shall have occasion, during the existence of the marital relation, to execute any deed, mortgage or other instrument dealing with or transferring any interest in real property belonging to the other, then the other shall join therein upon request for the purpose of releasing any dower, curtesy, and homestead interest in such property for the benefit of the other and of the grantee of such instrument, such instrument not to, however, impose any personal liability upon the party so joining in its execution for said purpose. Additionally, each of the parties agrees to execute any

other form or consent, at the request of the other party, if permitted by law, which may be required in order to effectuate the intent of this Agreement, including but not limited to a spousal waiver under the Federal Retirement Equity Act, it being understood, however, that even without the execution of a form or consent, the terms of this Agreement shall be controlling.

14. As long as they are permitted to do so by law, each party shall sign and file with the other joint Federal income tax returns and/or any applicable State and/or municipal income tax, capital gains, dividends or similar tax returns, provided that each party shall pay any and all taxes based upon the amounts of each's own taxable income, capital gains, dividends and/or the like, and further provided that neither party shall pay more taxes as a result of any such joint return than he or she would have paid if he or she filed separately as to such return. The parties shall divide any refunds, credits, and benefits reflected on or resulting from any such return on a proportionate basis in the same ratio as the total annual gross earned and unearned income of the Husband-to-be is to the total annual gross earned and unearned income of the Wife-to-be as reflected by such returns.

15. The parties agree that in the event that at any time during the existence of the marital relation between them if they should be or become residents of a state under the laws of which husband and wife acquire property interests commonly known as community property or marital property or any other property and interests different from the property interests of husband and wife under the current laws of the State of _____,

or the State of _____ adopts property laws similar to community property or marital property laws, then the parties' property interests shall nevertheless remain the same as they would have been under the terms and provisions of this Agreement construed in accordance with the current laws of the State of Connecticut; and the parties agree that they shall each at any time during or after the termination of the marital relation, make, execute, acknowledge and deliver any and all deeds and other instruments which shall be desirable or necessary to transfer any right, title or interest, in any property or estate of the other which a party may acquire by virtue of any so-called community property or marital property laws to the persons who would otherwise be entitled thereto by virtue of this Agreement.

16. This Agreement shall come into effect only if our contemplated marriage is solemnized and, upon coming into effect, this Agreement shall bind and inure to the benefit of us and our respective heirs, executors and administrators. If our contemplated marriage does not take place, this Agreement shall be in all respects and for all purposes null and void.

17. Each party shall, upon the request of the other, and/or the heirs, executors, administrators, conservators, assigns, representatives or the like of the other, forthwith execute, acknowledge and deliver a Separation Agreement setting forth the terms of this Agreement, in the event they cease living together after any such marriage, as well as any deeds, instruments, title papers and/or other documents that may be reasonably required to carry the intention of this Agreement into effect, including, but not limited to,

any and all such documents as may be required by the laws or the like of any jurisdiction, now in effect or hereafter enacted, which may affect the property rights of the parties as between themselves or with others. In the event either party brings any action for legal separation, dissolution of marriage, annulment, alimony, support, separate maintenance or the like, each party agrees he and she will submit this Agreement, and said Separation Agreement, if executed, to the Court before which such action was brought and shall seek incorporation by the Court of all terms of this Agreement, and said Separation Agreement, if executed, in any and all orders of said Court, whether pendente lite, interlocutory, final or otherwise.

18. The Husband-to-be sets forth in Schedule "A", and the Wife-to-be sets forth in Schedule "B", the statement of his and her respective income, assets, property, liabilities and/or the like, and each of them states and represents that his or her respective statement is complete, accurate, true, and correct, all as of the date of the execution of this Agreement.

19. This Agreement contains the entire understanding. There are no representations, warranties, promises, covenants or understandings, oral or otherwise, other than those expressly set forth herein. This Agreement shall be reviewed periodically by the parties but may be modified only by a written instrument executed by both of the parties in the same manner as this Agreement.

20. This Agreement shall be binding upon, and inure to the benefit of, the parties hereto and/or their respective heirs, executors, administrators, conservators, assigns, representatives and/or the like.

21. This Agreement shall be considered separable and, in the event any portion of this Agreement is declared void, invalid or unenforceable by any court of competent jurisdiction, the same shall not in any way affect any other portion or provision of this Agreement or the validity or enforceability of any such other portion or provision of this Agreement.

22. This Agreement may be executed in counterparts, each of which so executed shall be deemed an original, but all of which, taken together, shall constitute one and the same Agreement, binding upon us hereto, our heirs, executors, administrators, successors and permitted assigns.

23. All matters affecting the interpretation of this Agreement and our rights under this Agreement shall be governed by the current laws of the State of _____.

IN WITNESS WHEREOF, we have executed this Agreement on the day and year first above written.

IN THE PRESENCE OF:

_____

_____   _____

_____

_____   _____

I, (NAME OF W's ATTORNEY), of the law firm of _____, hereby acknowledge that I reviewed the contents of the above Prenuptial Agreement with (NAME).

I, (NAME OF H's ATTORNEY), of the law firm of _____, hereby acknowledge that I reviewed the contents of the above Prenuptial Agreement with (NAME).

_____   _____

(NAME OF W's ATTORNEY)   (NAME OF H's ATTORNEY)

STATE OF _____)

　　　　　　　　　　　　　　) ss. _____, 2008

COUNTY OF _____)

　　　On this　　　　day of　　　　　, 200_, before me, personally appeared　　　　　　　　, one of the signers and sealers of the foregoing instrument, and acknowledged the same to be her free and voluntary act and deed.

_____

　　　　　　　Commissioner of the Superior Court

STATE OF _____)

) ss. _____, 2008

COUNTY OF _____)

 On this day of   , 200_, before me, personally appeared   , one of the signers and sealers of the foregoing instrument, and acknowledged the same to be his free and voluntary act and deed.

_____

     Commissioner of the Superior Court

APPENDIX B
Tripartite Document (*Shelo le-Halakhah*)

Jewish Prenuptial Agreement

This document is to certify that on _____ day of the month of _____in the year 20__, in the City of _____, State of _____, the groom _____, and the bride _____, of their own free will and accord entered into the following agreement with respect to their intended marriage.

The groom made the following declaration to the bride under the *huppah*_(wedding canopy):

"I will betroth and marry you according to the laws of Moses and the people of Israel, subject to the following conditions:

"If I return to live in our marital home with you present at least once every fifteen months until either you or I die, then our betrothal (*kiddushin*) and our marriage (*nisu'in*) shall remain valid and binding;

"But if I am absent from our joint marital home for fifteen months continuously for whatever reason, even by duress, then our betrothal (*kiddushin*) and our marriage (*nisu'in*) will have been null and void. Our conduct should be like unmarried people sharing a residence, and the blessings recited a nullity.

"I acknowledge that I have effected the above obligation by means of a *quinyan* (formal Jewish transaction) before a *beit din hashuv* (esteemed rabbinical court) as mandated by Jewish law. The above condition is made in accordance with the laws of the Torah, as derived from Numbers Chapter 32. Even a sexual relationship between us shall not void this condition. My wife shall be believed like one hundred witnesses to testify that I have never voided this condition.

"Should a Jewish divorce be required of me for whatever reason, I also appoint anyone who will see my signature on this form to act as scribe (*sofer*) to acquire pen, ink and feather for me and write a *Get* (a Jewish Document of Divorce), one or more, to divorce with it my wife, and he should write the *Get lishmi*, especially for me, *ve-lishmah*, especially for her, *u'lesheim gerushin*, and for the purpose of divorce. I herewith command any two witnesses who see my signature on this form to act as witnesses to the bill of divorce (*Get*) to sign as witnesses on the *Get* that the above-mentioned scribe will write. They should sign *lishmi*, especially for me, *ve-lishmah*, and especially for her, *u'leshem gerushin*, and for the purpose of divorce, to divorce with it my abovementioned wife. I herewith command anyone who sees my signature on this form to act as my agent to take the *Get*, after it is written and signed, and be my messenger to give it into the hands of my wife whenever she so wishes. His hand should be like my hand, his giving like my giving, his mouth like my mouth, and I give him authority to appoint another messenger in his place, and that messenger another messenger, one messenger after another, even to one hundred messengers, of his own free will, even to appoint someone not is his presence, until the *Get*, the document of divorce, reaches her hands, and as soon as the *Get* reaches her hands from his hands or from his messenger's hands, or from his messenger's messenger's hands, even to one hundred messengers, she shall be divorced by it from me and be allowed to any man. My permission is given to the rabbi in charge to make such changes in the writings of the names as he sees fit. I undertake with all seriousness, even with an oath of the Torah, that I will not nullify the effectiveness of the *Get*, the Jewish Document of Divorce, to divorce my wife or the power of the above-mentioned messenger to deliver it to my wife. And I nullify any kind of a statement that I may have made which could hurt the effectiveness of the *Get* to divorce my wife or the effectiveness of the above-mentioned messenger to deliver it to my wife. Even if my wife and I should continue to reside together after the providing of this authorization to divorce her, and even if we have a sexual relationship after this authorization to write, sign and deliver a *Get*, such a sexual relationship should not be construed as implicitly or explicitly nullifying this authorization to write, sign and deliver a *Get*. My wife shall be believed like one hundred witnesses to testify that I have not nullified my authorization to appoint the scribe to write the *Get* on my behalf, or the witnesses to sign the *Get* on my behalf or any messenger to deliver it to the hand of my wife.

"Furthermore I recognize that my wife has agreed to marry me only with the understanding that should she wish to be divorced that I would give a *Get* within fifteen months of her requesting such a bill of divorce. I recognize that should I decline to give such a *Get* for whatever reason (even a reason based on my duress), I have violated the agreement that is the predicate for our marriage, and I consent for our marriage to be labeled a nullity based on the decree of our community that all marriages ought to end with a *Get* given within fifteen months. We both belong to a community where the majority of the great rabbis and the *batei din* of that community have authorized the use of annulment in cases like this, and I accept the communal decree on this matter as binding upon me.

"Furthermore, should this agreement be deemed ineffective as a matter of *halakhah* (Jewish law) at any time, we would not have married at all.

"I announce now that no witness, including any future testimony I might provide, shall be believed to nullify this document or any provision herein."

Signature of Groom _____

The bride replied to the groom:

"I consent to the conditions you have made and I accept the *qinyan* (formal Jewish transaction) in front of the *beit din hashuv* (esteemed rabbinical court)."

Signature of Bride _____

We the undersigned duly constituted *beit din* witnessed the oral statements and signatures of the groom and bride.

Rabbi _____

Witness _____

Witness _____

APPENDIX C
Nonmarital Cohabitation / Living Together Agreement

AGREEMENT made this _____ day of _____, 20___, by and between _____ _____, "First Party", and _____ _____, "Second Party".

WHEREAS the parties are presently residing with each other at _____ _____, have been doing so since _____ _____ and intend to continue living together in this arrangement;

WHEREAS the parties desire to affix and define their respective property rights and liabilities arising from their joint residency;

WHEREAS the parties each acknowledge that they enter into this agreement voluntarily, without any duress or undue influence, and that each has had the opportunity to consult with counsel of his/her choice;

THE PARTIES HEREBY AGREE:

I. **Marital Status.** The joint residency of the parties shall in no way render the parties married, by operation of common law or any other operation of law.

2. **Consideration.** Consideration for this Agreement consists solely of the mutual promises herein contained and the mutual promises of each party to act as the living companion and partner to the other. This Agreement fully contemplates and compensates any and all services provided by either party for the benefit of the other during the course of their joint residency. The furnishing of sexual services shall in no way be construed as consideration for this Agreement.

3. **Disclosure of Current Financial Status.** Each party has fully and completely, to the best of his/her knowledge, disclosed to the other party his/her current financial condition including all assets and liabilities. Each party has attached a balance sheet to this agreement indicating his/her current assets and liabilities with the understanding that this balance sheet reflects his/her current financial status to the best of his/her ability.

4. **Division of Living Expenses.** Necessary and jointly approved living expenses shall be apportioned between the parties as follows:

The First Party shall contribute _____ percent (_____%) per month;

The Second Party shall contribute _____ percent (_____%) per month.

The parties shall deposit their pro rata contributions monthly into the joint checking account of the parties. Either party may draw upon this checking account. Any property purchased from this checking account shall be considered joint property of the parties, owned according to the respective party's percentage of contribution stated above.

5. **Separate Property.** The parties shall keep the following properties as the separate property of the recipient and said properties shall not be subject to division at the termination of this Agreement:

(a) Individual earnings, salary or wages acquired before or after the execution of this Agreement;

(b) Individual gifts, bequests, devises or inheritances acquired before or after the execution of this Agreement;

(c) All property, real or personal, owned by a party at the date of execution of this Agreement;

(d) All income or proceeds derived from the aforementioned properties.

6. **Joint Property.** All property acquired by the parties after the execution date of this Agreement and before the termination of this Agreement and procured jointly with joint resources and funds shall be considered joint property of the parties with each party possessing his/her aforementioned percentage of ownership.

7. **Commingling of Property.** Absent a reasonable demonstration of sole ownership, where either party commingles joint property with separate property, any commingled property shall be presumed to be joint property of the parties.

8. **Division of Property upon Termination.** Upon termination of this Agreement or termination of the joint residency, all jointly owned property shall be divided

among the parties according to their pro rata share listed above. If the parties are unable to agree on the appropriate division of joint property, they may appoint an independent and mutually agreed upon Third-party to act as Appraiser. The Appraiser shall divide the property among the parties according to his/her pro rata share.

9. **Duty of Good Faith.** This Agreement creates a fiduciary relationship between the parties in which each party agrees to act with the utmost of good faith and fair dealing toward the other in the management of their joint property and in all other aspects of this Agreement.

10. **Legal Names of Parties.** Each party shall retain his/her legal name, including surname, as printed and signed in this Agreement.

11. **Duration of Agreement.** This Agreement shall become effective at the date of execution and shall remain in effect until termination. Termination shall be effected by written notice by either party, cessation of the joint residency by either party or death of either party. Either party may terminate this Agreement unilaterally at any time.

12. **Death of Party.** Upon the death of either party, the surviving party waives all rights to support by the deceased party.

13. **Complete Agreement.** It is the intent of the parties that this Agreement be the full and complete agreement between the parties regarding their joint residency. There are no other agreements between the parties regarding their joint residency other than those stated herein. This Agreement shall only be modified by a writing executed by both parties hereto.

14. **Severability of Provisions.** Should any paragraph or provision of this Agreement be held invalid, void, or otherwise unenforceable, it is the intent of the parties that the remaining portions shall nevertheless continue in full force and effect without impairment.

15. **Governing Law.** This Agreement shall be governed by, interpreted and construed in accordance with the laws of the State of _____.

IN WITNESS WHEREOF , the parties have executed this Agreement at _____ on this _____ day of _____, 20___.

_____

First Party

_____

Second Party

_____

Witness

_____

Witness

APPENDIX D
Postnuptial Agreement

THIS AGREEMENT is made between HUSBAND (or "husband") and WIFE (or "wife"),

WHEREAS the parties were married on _____ *and* have since that date been living as husband and wife, and

WHEREAS, the parties wish to amend the or Agreement in order to reflect certain charges in their relationship, and

WHEREAS, the parties, with the assistant of separate and independent legal counsel, have each fully considered their respective financial conditions, their existing rights and obligations and the rights and obligations which but for the Prior Agreement would accrue to each other because of their relationship Husband and Wife, and

WHREAS, except as otherwise expressly provided in this Agreement, HUSBAND desires to keep all of his property now owned or hereafter acquired, free from any claim.   WIFE might otherwise acquire by reason of the or by reason of her surviving him his widow, and

WHEREAS, except otherwise expressly provided in this Agreement, WIFE desires to keep all of her property now owned or hereafter acquired, free from any claim that HUSBAND might otherwise acquire by reason of the marriage or by reason of his surviving her as her widower.

It is therefore agreed:

I. **Release of Marital Rights by Husband in the Event of Death of Wife.**

(a) HUSBAND hereby waives and releases all right and interest, statutory or otherwise, including, but not limited to courtesy, dower, widower's allowance, statutory allowance, distribution in intestacy, pretermitted spouse, exempt spouse, homestead and statutory share under the laws of any jurisdiction (whether in the form of a right to elect against WIFE's Will or to treat a lifetime conveyance for the other parts as testamentary or otherwise), which he might acquire by reason of the marriage to or the husband, widower, heir at law, next of kin or distributee of WIFE, in her property, owned by her at the time of the marriage or acquired by her at any time thereafter (whether by inheritance or otherwise) and in her estate upon her death, regardless of changes in circumstances that may occur over tire.

HUSBAND also waives the right to contest the admission and probate of WIFE's Will. HUSBAND acknowledges that WIFE has no obligation to provide for him in her Will, HUSBAND agrees not to petition to be appointed as a fiduciary of WIFE's estate unless specifically named as such in her Will.

(c) HUSBAND also waives and releases any and all claims and rights which he may have or acquire in any pension, profit sharing, deferred compensation, 4 0 1 (k) or other employee benefit of WIFE whether qualified or nonqualified for federal tax purposes and whether such interest arises by contract, pursuant to said plan or by the Retirement Equity Act of 1984 or otherwise and a g r e e s immediately upon demand to execute any or documents necessary to effectuate this provision and to release any such interest.

Release of Marital Rights *by Wife* **in the Event of Death of Husband.**

(a) WIFE hereby waives and releases all right and interest, statutory or *otherwise,* including, *but not* limited *to, curtesy, dower, widow's allowance,* statutory allowance, distribution in intestacy, pretermitted spouse, exempt property, homestead and statutory share under the laws of any jurisdiction (whether in the form of a fight to elect against HUSBAND'S Will or to treat a lifetime conveyance for the other party as testamentary or otherwise), which she might acquire by reason of the marriage to, or as the Wife, widow, heir at law, next of kin or distribute of HUSBAND, in his property, owned by him at the time of the marriage or acquired by at anytime thereafter (whether by inheritance or otherwise) and in his estate upon his death, regardless of changes in circumstances that may occur over time.

(b) WIFE also waives the right to contest the admission and probate of HUSBAND'S Will. WIFE acknowledges that HUSBAND has no obligation to provide for her in his Will. WIFE agrees not to petition to be appointed as a fiduciary of HUSBAND's estate unless specifically named as such fiduciary in his Will.

3. **Separate Property.**

(a) Except provided in this Agreement, the parties agree that each shall keep and retain sole and separate ownership, control and enjoyment of all property, real and personal and wheresoever situated, which he or she now owns, or which may hereafter be acquired by either of them in any manner whatsoever, including any and all increases in value, including increases in value due to the efforts or contributions of the other party. Without limiting the generality of this Paragraph 3 the parties agree that each shall hold all such property, free from any claim, lien or right, inchoate or otherwise, on the part of the other and that each party may dispose of any part or all of such property, at any time or times and in any manner as he or she may see f except as may be provided for herein.

(b) Except as otherwise provided in this Agreement, and without limiting the foregoing. the parties agree that the following (i.e. all of this Paragraph 3(b)) is the separate property of each party, exempt from equitable distribution, and shall remain her or his separate property under her or his control and ownership, including and all increases in value, including increases in value due to the efforts or contributions of the other and shall at no time become marital property:

(I) <u>Earnings and Income</u>. Earnings and income accumulated as a result of party's skill, efforts; education, background, personal services, invest en and work together with all property acquired or income derived therefrom, will be the separate property of the party who earned the income or though whose income said property was obtained. Each party hereto acknowledges that but for this agreement, the earnings and accumulations from the services, skills and efforts of one of the parties might deemed to constitute marital property, and that by this Agreement such earnings, income and other accumulated properties are specifically designated the separate property of the person to whom the earnings, income and accumulations are attributable.

(2) Assets, The property described hereafter shall remain the separate property of each party:

    (i) all property, whether real or personal, belonging to each party at the commencement of their marriage;

    (ii) all property acquired by each party out of the proceeds or income from property owned at the commencement of the marriage, or attributable to appreciation in value of said property, whether the enhancement is due to market conditions or to the services, skills or efforts of either paw to this Agreement;

    (iii) all property hereafter acquired by each party, including all property hereafter acquired by gift, devise, bequest or inheritance.

(3) <u>Specific Assets.</u> Without limiting the foregoing, the parties acknowledge that the following constitutes a partial list of specific items of separate property currently belonging to each party:

HUSBAND

See Exhibit "A " attached

WIFE

See Exhibit "B" attached

    (i) Interest and investments in corporations, and in partnerships, including without limitation those set forth in Exhibits "A" and "B" attached hereto.

(ii) All earnings and accumulations from HUSBAND's business endeavors, as well as machinery, furnishings, office supplies and equipment purchased either prior to or during the marriage for use in connection with them.

(c) The parties specifically acknowledge and agree that any marital residence acquired prior to the marriage, so long as it is not acquired or held in WIFE'S name individually, will not to any extent be considered her separate property or marital property of the parties, notwithstanding any tangible or intangible contribution to the value thereof by WIFE. WIFE understands and agrees that, accordingly, any such marital residence is exempt from equitable distribution. Further, any such marital residence is not subject to any claim, lien or right on her part, except as expressly provided in this Agreement.

5. <u>Transfers Between the Parties</u>

Each party shall have the right to transfer or convey to the other any property or interest therein which may be lawfully conveyed or transferred during his or her lifetime or by Will or otherwise upon death, and neither party intends by this Agreement to limit or restrict in any way the right and power to receive any such transfer or conveyance from the other.

6. **<u>Provision for Support of WIFE</u>**

(a) Notwithstanding Paragraph 2(b) hereof, in. the event of the death of HUSBAND while the parties are marred to and living with, each other as husband and wife, or in the event of the dissolution of their marriage or legal separation from each other, then HUSBAND shall provide, or cause to be provided, a cash bequest or payment to WIFE in the amount of $_____.

(b) In the event of the dissolution of their marriage or legal separation from each other, HUSBAND shall provide, or cause to provided, to WIFE, free of any thereon, on or about the first day of each month after such proceedings have been commenced, whether by service of a complaint or otherwise, the sum of $_____ until such proceedings are either withdrawn or a final dissolution of their marriage has been entered.

7. Provision for Support of the Issue of Wife and Husband

(a) In addition to the monthly payments provided in Paragraph 7 above, HUSBAND shall provide, or cause to be provided to WIFE, in the event of the dissolution of their marriage, or legal separation from each other, whether by service of a complaint or otherwise, on or about the first day of each month after such proceedings have been commenced, as and for the support and maintenance of each unemancipated child of the marriage of WIFE and HUSBAND ("Child") the sum of $_____ per month, per child.

8. Testamentary Provision for WIFE

In the event of the death of HUSBAND while the parties are married to and living with each other as husband and. wife, in addition to the provisions of Paragraphs 2(b) and 7(a), HUSBAND agrees to provide WIFE one-third (1/3) of the residue of his estate before estate and inheritance taxes but after payments of debts and expenses, specific bequests, legacies, devises and charitable bequests not to exceed additional ten percent (10%) of the gross.

9. Dissolution of Marriage

(a) The parties intend that their marriage will last for as long as they both live. They wish, however, to establish their respective rights and obligations with respect to alimony and distribution of property in the event of a dissolution of their marriage or legal separation. The parties believe that each of them has sufficient property and/or earring power to provide for his or her own support both now and, to the extent currently foreseeable, in the future, taking into account insofar as WIFE is concerned the obligations of HUSBAND hereunder.

Acquisition of property in joint name during the term of the marriage shall be deemed a gift from one party to the other.

(a) All property separately held, regardless of its value before, during or after the marriage, will remain the property of its separate owner in accordance with Paragraph 3 of this Ageement, subject, however, to the provisions of Paragraph 5 of this Agreement.

(b) Neither party intends hereby this Agreement, to discharge any obligation of the other with respect to the support of any children born of the marriage.

(c) In the event of any decree of dissolution or divorce, this Agreement shall survive such decree of dissolution or divorce and shall not merge therein.

10. **Necessary Documents**

Each party shall, upon the request of the other, execute, acknowledge, and deliver any additional instruments that reasonably may be required to carry the intention of this Agreement into effect, including such instruments as may be required by the laws of any jurisdiction, now in effect or hereafter enacted, which may affect the property rights of the parties as between themselves or with others.

12. Disclosure of Assets

Each of the parties represents and warrants to the other that he or she is aware of the nature and extent of the property of the other and has carefully read and understands this Agreement and is fully cognizant of its terms. Each party agrees to provide to the other upon request copies of any income tax return for the past three years. Each of the parties understands that by executing this Agreement he or she is irrevocably barring property rights of very substantial value which might otherwise accrue to him or her by virtue of their marriage and has freely decided, after mature reflection and deliberation, and after having been fully advised of such rights by counsel, that he or she wishes to enter into this Agreement.

13. Liability for Debts.

Any and all debts contracted by either party before or subsequent to the marriage of the parties are to be the separate obligation of the party who shall have contracted such debts, and the other party shall not be liable for payment thereof.

14. **Independent Counsel.**

Each party has been advised by separate independent counsel of his or her own selection in connection with the execution of this Agreement:

15. **Effective Date**

This Agreement shall take effect upon the signing of this Agreement by the parties.

16. **Consideration**

The consideration for this Agreement is the mutual promises contained herein.

17. **Completeness and Mofidications.**

This Agreement contains the entire understanding of the parties, and no representations or promises have been made except as contained herein. This Agreement may not be modified or amended except by written instrument signed by the parties hereto.

18. **Benefit.**

This Agreement shall bind and insure to the benefit of the parties and their respective legal representatives, successors, heirs and assigns.

19. **Applicable Law**

This Agreement shall be construed in all respects under the laws of the State of _____.

20. **Titles.**

The title of each paragraph of is agreement is included for purposes of identification only and shall not be used to construe any provision contained this agreement or for any other reason.

21. <u>Severability</u>

In the event any provision of this Agreement shall held to be illegal, invalid or void, for any reason whatsoever, by any court of competent jurisdiction and such declaration shall tae upheld on any and all appeals taken therefrom, this Agreement shall be read if such illegal, invalid or void provision were not a part hereof.

In all other respects, the Prior Agreement is ratified and reaffirmed by the parties. In the event of a conflict between the provisions of the Prior Agreement and this Agreement, the terms of this Agreement shall control, and prevail.

22. <u>Counterparts.</u>

This Agreement may executed in two or more counterparts, each of which, or a facsimile copy thereof, shall be deemed to be an original, but all of which shall constitute one and the same instrument.

APPENDIX E

NAME:			DATE:	
SWORN FINANCIAL AFFIDAVIT				
I.		MONTHLY INCOME		
	A.	Monthly Income from Principal Employment		
		Employer name/address:		
		Gross monthly wages		
		Less deductions:		
		Federal taxes		
		State taxes		
		FICA		
		Medicare		
		Medical insurance		
		Dental insurance		
		401(k)		
		Other (describe)		
		Total deductions:		
		Net Monthly Wages		

	B.	<u>All Other Income</u> (include in-kind compensation, gratuities, rents, interest, dividends, pension, etc.)			
		<u>TOTAL NET MONTHLY INCOME</u> <u>ALL SOURCES</u>			
II.		<u>BASIC MONTHLY</u> <u>EXPENSES</u>			
	A.	<u>Primary Residence</u>			
		Mortgage or rent (circle one)			
		Real estate taxes			
		Common chgs./assoc. dues			
		Homeowner's insurance			
		Electricity			
		Gas			
		Heating fuel			
		Firewood			
		Water			
		Telephone (land & cell)			
		Trash collection			
		Cable/Internet			
		Home repairs/ maintenance			
		Yard maint./plowing, etc.			
		Security system			

		Cleaning service			
		Misc. household supplies			
	B.	Insurance - Costs not Covered by Employer			
		(List amounts, carriers and individuals covered under policy)			
	C.	Unreimbursed Health Expenses			
		(List amounts and individuals covered under policy)			
		Medical			
		Dental/orthodontia			
		Pharmacy			
		Therapy			
	D.	Food			
		Groceries			
		Restaurants			
		Liquor and wine			
	E.	Clothing			
		Self			
		Child(ren)			

	F.	Household			
		Dry cleaning/laundry			
		Newspaper/stationery			
		Books/CDs/videos			
		Pet care			
	G.	Personal			
		Cosmetics/personal grooming			
		Hairdresser/barber			
		Tax preparation			
	H.	Transportation			
		Gas and oil			
		Auto loan/lease			
		Insurance and license			
		Repairs and maintenance			
		Personal property tax			
		Parking			
		Tolls			
	I.	Child(ren)			
		Babysitters/day care			
		Toys/games			
		Camp			
		Educational expenses			
		Hairdresser/barber			
		Sports lessons/equipment			
		Books, fees, etc.			
		Tutor			

	J.	Charities and Dues			
		(List club/membership names and amounts)			
	K.	Entertainment and Vacations			
		Entertainment			
		Trips and vacations			
	L.	Gifts			
		Holiday gifts			
		Birthday gifts			
		Other gifts			
	M.	Support Paid			
		Alimony			
		Child support			
		College			
	N.	Other Expenses			
		(Include monthly payments on recurrent debt from Section III)			

TOTAL BASIC MONTHLY EXPENSES					
III.	LIABILITIES				
	(List outstanding liability balances & whether ea. liability is held solely or jointly)				
TOTAL LIABILITIES					
IV.	ASSETS				
	A.	Real Estate (reflect whether owned solely or jointly)			
		Address:			
		Value			
		Mortgage			
		Net equity			

		One-half equity (if applicable)			
		Address:			
		Value			
		Mortgage			
		Net equity			
		One-half equity (if applicable)			
	B.	Motor Vehicles (reflect whether owned solely or jointly)			
		Year / make / model:			
		Value			
		Loan			
		Net equity			
		One-half equity (if applicable)			
		Year / make / model:			
		Value			
		Loan			
		Net equity			
		One-half equity (if applicable)			
	C.	Other Personal Property (reflect whether owned solely or jointly)			

	D.	Bank Accounts (list amounts and reflect whether held solely or jointly)			
	E.	Brokerage Accounts/Other Securities (list amounts and reflect whether held solely or jointly)			
	F.	Insurance (list company and cash value amount)			
	G.	Retirement / Pension Accounts			

	H.	<u>All Other Assets</u> (reflect whether owned solely or jointly)			
		Furniture			
		Jewelry			
		Artwork			
		Electronic equipment			
<u>TOTAL CASH VALUE ALL ASSETS</u>					
V.		<u>SUMMARY</u>			
	I.	Total Net Monthly Income All Sources			
	II.	Total Basic Monthly Expenses			
	III.	Total Liabilities			
	IV.	Total Cash Value All Assets			
VI.		<u>CERTIFICATION</u>			
	I hereby certify that the foregoing statement is accurate to the best of my				
	knowledge and that I can, if requested, submit documentation for all assets,				

		liabilities and expenses listed above.			
			_____ _____		
Subscribed and sworn to before me this					
_____ day of _____, 200_					
_____ _____					
Commissioner of the Superior Court					

UNIFORM PREMARITAL AGREEMENT ACT

Drafted by the

NATIONAL CONFERENCE OF COMMISSIONERS

ON UNIFORM STATE LAWS

and by it

APPROVED AND RECOMMENDED FOR ENACTMENT

IN ALL THE STATES

at its

ANNUAL CONFERENCE

MEETING IN ITS NINETY-SECOND YEAR

IN BOCA RATON, FLORIDA

JULY 22 - 29, 1983

WITH PREFATORY NOTE AND COMMENTS

UNIFORM PREMARITAL AGREEMENT ACT

The Committee that acted for the National Conference of Commissioners on Uniform State Laws in preparing the Uniform Premarital Agreement Act was as follows:

Advisor to Special Committee on Uniform Premarital Agreement Act

MARJORIE A. O'CONNELL, *American Bar Association*

Final, approved copies of this Act and copies of all Uniform and Model Acts and other printed matter issued by the Conference may be obtained from:

NATIONAL CONFERENCE OF COMMISSIONERS

ON UNIFORM STATE LAWS

645 North Michigan Avenue, Suite 510

Chicago, Illinois 60611

(312) 321-9710

UNIFORM PREMARITAL AGREEMENT ACT

PREFATORY NOTE

The number of marriages between persons previously married and the number of marriages between persons each of whom is intending to continue to pursue a career is steadily increasing. For these and other reasons, it is becoming more and more common for persons contemplating marriage to seek to resolve by agreement certain issues presented by the forthcoming marriage. However, despite a lengthy legal history for these premarital agreements, there is a substantial uncertainty as to the enforceability of all, or a portion, of the provisions of these agreements and a significant lack of uniformity of treatment of these agreements among the states. The problems caused by this uncertainty and nonuniformity are greatly exacerbated by the mobility of our population. Nevertheless, this uncertainty and nonuniformity seem reflective not so much of basic policy differences between the states but rather a result of spasmodic, reflexive response to varying factual circumstances at different times. Accordingly, uniform legislation conforming to modern social policy which provides both certainty and sufficient flexibility to accommodate different circumstances would appear to be both a significant improvement and a goal realistically capable of achievement.

This Act is intended to be relatively limited in scope. Section 1 defines a "premarital agreement" as "an agreement between prospective spouses made in contemplation of marriage and to be effective upon marriage." Section 2 requires that a premarital agreement be in writing and signed by both parties. Section 4 provides that a premarital agreement becomes effective upon the marriage of the parties. These sections establish significant parameters. That is, the Act does not deal with agreements between persons who live together but who do not contemplate marriage or who do not marry. Nor does the Act provide for postnuptial or separation agreements or with oral agreements.

On the other hand, agreements which are embraced by the act are permitted to deal with a wide variety of matters and Section 3 provides an **illustrative** list of those matters, including spousal support, which may properly be dealt with in a premarital agreement.

Section 6 is the key operative section of the Act and sets forth the conditions under which a premarital agreement is not enforceable. An agreement is not enforceable if the party against whom enforcement is sought proves that (a) he or she did not execute the agreement voluntarily or that (b) the agreement was unconscionable when it was executed and, before execution of the agreement, he or she (1) was not provided a fair and reasonable disclosure of the property or financial obligations of the other party, (2) did not voluntarily and expressly waive, in writing, any right to disclosure of the property or financial obligations of the other party beyond the disclosure provided, **and** (3) did not have, or reasonably could not have had, an adequate knowledge of the property and financial obligations of the other party.

Even if these conditions are not proven, if a provision of a premarital agreement modifies or eliminates spousal support, and that modification or elimination would cause a party to be eligible for support under a program of public assistance at the time of separation, marital dissolution, or death, a court is authorized to order the other party to provide support to the extent necessary to avoid that eligibility.

These sections form the heart of the Act; the remaining sections deal with more tangential issues. Section 5 prescribes the manner in which a premarital agreement may be amended or revoked; Section 7 provides for very limited enforcement where a marriage is subsequently determined to be void; and Section 8 tolls any statute of limitations applicable to an action asserting a claim for relief under a premarital agreement during the parties' marriage.

UNIFORM PREMARITAL AGREEMENT ACT

SECTION 1. DEFINITIONS. As used in this Act:

(1) "Premarital agreement" means an agreement between prospective spouses made in contemplation of marriage and to be effective upon marriage.

(2) "Property" means an interest, present or future, legal or equitable, vested or contingent, in real or personal property, including income and earnings.

Comment

The definition of "premarital agreement" set forth in subsection (1) is limited to an agreement between prospective spouses made in contemplation of and to be effective upon marriage. Agreements between persons living together but not contemplating marriage (see *Marvin v. Marvin*, 18 Cal. 3d 660 (1976), judgment after trial modified, 122 Cal. App. 3d 871 (1981)) and postnuptial or separation agreements are outside the scope of this Act. Formal requirements are prescribed by Section 2. An illustrative list of matters which may be included in an agreement is set forth in Section 3.

Subsection (2) is designed to embrace all forms of property and interests therein. These may include rights in a professional license or practice, employee benefit plans, pension and retirement accounts, and so on. The reference to income or earnings includes both income from property and earnings from personal services.

SECTION 2. FORMALITIES. A premarital agreement must be in writing and signed by both parties. It is enforceable without consideration.

Comment

This section restates the common requirement that a premarital agreement be reduced to writing and signed by both parties (see Ariz. Rev. Stats. § 25-201; Ark. Stats. § 55-310; Cal. Civ. C. § 5134; 13 Dela. Code 1974 § 301; Idaho Code § 32-917; Ann. Laws Mass. ch. 209, § 25; Minn. Stats. Ann. § 519.11; Montana Rev. C. § 36-123; New Mex Stats. Ann. 1978 40-2-4; Ore. Rev. Stats. § 108.140;

Vernon's Texas Codes Ann. § 5.44; Vermont Stats. Ann. Title 12, § 181). Many states also require other formalities, including notarization or an acknowledgement (see, e.g., Arizona, Arkansas, California, Idaho, Montana, New Mexico) but may then permit the formal statutory requirement to be avoided or satisfied subsequent to execution (see *In re Marriage of Cleveland*, 76 Cal. App. 3d 357 (1977) (premarital agreement never acknowledged but "proved" by sworn testimony of parties in dissolution proceeding)). This act dispenses with all formal requirements except a writing signed by both parties. Although the section is framed in the singular, the agreement may consist of one or more documents intended to be part of the agreement and executed as required by this section.

Section 2 also restates what appears to be the almost universal rule regarding the marriage as consideration for a premarital agreement (see, e.g., Ga. Code § 20-303; *Barnhill v. Barnhill*, 386 So. 2d 749 (Ala. Civ. App. 1980); *Estate of Gillilan v. Estate of Gillilan*, 406 N.E. 2d 981 (Ind. App. 1980); *Friedlander v. Friedlander*, 494 P.2d 208 (Wash. 1972); but cf. *Wilson v. Wilson*, 170 A. 2d 679, 685 (Me. 1961)). The primary importance of this rule has been to provide a degree of mutuality of benefits to support the enforceability of a premarital agreement. A marriage is a prerequisite for the effectiveness of a premarital agreement under this act (see Section 4). This requires that there be a ceremonial marriage. Even if this marriage is subsequently determined to have been void, Section 7 may provide limits of enforceability of an agreement entered into in contemplation of that marriage. Consideration as such is not required and the standards for enforceability are established by Sections 6 and 7. Nevertheless, this provision is retained here as a desirable, if not essential, restatement of the law. On the other hand, the fact that marriage is deemed to be consideration for the purpose of this act does not change the rules applicable in other areas of law (see, e.g., 26 U.S.C.A. § 2043 (release of certain marital rights not treated as consideration for federal estate tax), 2512; *Merrill v. Fahs*, 324 U.S. 308, rehearing denied 324 U.S. 888 (release of marital rights in premarital agreement not adequate and full consideration for purposes of federal gift tax).

Finally, a premarital agreement is a contract. As required for any other contract, the parties must have the capacity to contract in order to enter into a binding agreement. Those persons who lack the capacity to contract but who under other provisions of law are permitted to enter into a binding agreement may enter into a premarital agreement under those other provisions of law.

SECTION 3. CONTENT.

(a) Parties to a premarital agreement may contract with respect to:

(1) the rights and obligations of each of the parties in any of the property of either or both of them whenever and wherever acquired or located;

1982); *Parniawski v. Parniawski*, 359 A.2d 719 (Conn. 1976); *Volid v. Volid*, 286 N.E. 2d 42 (Ill. 1972); *Osborne v. Osborne*, 428 N.E. 2d 810 (Mass. 1981); *Hudson v. Hudson*, 350 P.2d 596 (Okla. 1960); *Unander v. Unander*, 506 P.2d 719 (Ore. 1973)) (see Sections 7 and 8).

Paragraph (8) of subsection (a) makes clear that the parties may also contract with respect to other matters, including personal rights and obligations, not in violation of public policy or a criminal statute. Hence, subject to this limitation, an agreement may provide for such matters as the choice of abode, the freedom to pursue career opportunities, the upbringing of children, and so on. However, subsection (b) of this section makes clear that an agreement may not adversely affect what would otherwise be the obligation of a party to a child.

SECTION 4. EFFECT OF MARRIAGE. A premarital agreement becomes effective upon marriage.

Comment

This section establishes a marriage as a prerequisite for the effectiveness of a premarital agreement. As a consequence, the act does not provide for a situation where persons live together without marrying. In that situation, the parties must look to the other law of the jurisdiction (see *Marvin v. Marvin*, 18 Cal. 3d 660 (1976); judgment after trial modified, 122 Cal. App. 3d 871 (1981)).

SECTION 5. AMENDMENT, REVOCATION. After marriage, a premarital agreement may be amended or revoked only by a written agreement signed by the parties. The amended agreement or the revocation is enforceable without consideration.

Comment

This section requires the same formalities of execution for an amendment or revocation of a premarital agreement as are required for its original execution (cf. *Estate of Gillilan v. Estate of Gillilan*, 406 N.E. 2d 981 (Ind. App. 1980) (agreement may be altered by subsequent agreement but not simply by inconsistent acts).

SECTION 6. ENFORCEMENT.

(a) A premarital agreement is not enforceable if the party against whom enforcement is sought proves that:

(1) that party did not execute the agreement voluntarily; or

(2) the agreement was unconscionable when it was executed and, before execution of the agreement, that party:

(i) was not provided a fair and reasonable disclosure of the property or financial obligations of the other party;

(ii) did not voluntarily and expressly waive, in writing, any right to disclosure of the property or financial obligations of the other party beyond the disclosure provided; and

(iii) did not have, or reasonably could not have had, an adequate knowledge of the property or financial obligations of the other party.

(b) If a provision of a premarital agreement modifies or eliminates spousal support and that modification or elimination causes one party to the agreement to be eligible for support under a program of public assistance at the time of separation or marital dissolution, a court, notwithstanding the terms of the agreement, may require the other party to provide support to the extent necessary to avoid that eligibility.

(c) An issue of unconscionability of a premarital agreement shall be decided by the court as a matter of law.

Comment

This section sets forth the conditions which must be proven to avoid the enforcement of a premarital agreement. If prospective spouses enter into a premarital agreement and their subsequent marriage is determined to be void, the enforceability of the agreement is governed by Section 7.

The conditions stated under subsection (a) are comparable to concepts which are expressed in the statutory and decisional law of many jurisdictions. Enforcement based on disclosure and voluntary execution is perhaps most common (see, e.g., Ark. Stats. § 55-309; Minn. Stats. Ann. § 519.11; *In re Kaufmann's Estate*, 171 A. 2d 48 (Pa. 1961) (alternate holding)). However, knowledge or reason to know, together with voluntary execution, may also be sufficient (see, e.g., Tenn. Code Ann. § 36-606; *Barnhill v. Barnhill*, 386 So. 2d 749 (Ala. Civ. App. 1980); *Del Vecchio v. Del Vecchio*, 143 So. 2d 17 (Fla. 1962); *Coward and Coward*, 582 P. 2d 834 (Or. App. 1978); but see *Matter of Estate of Lebsock*, 618 P.2d 683 (Colo. App. 1980)) and so may a voluntary, knowing waiver (see *Hafner v. Hafner*, 295 N.W. 2d 567 (Minn. 1980)). In each of these situations, it should be underscored that execution must have been voluntary (see *Lutgert v. Lutgert*, 338 So. 2d 1111 (Fla. 1976); see also 13 Dela. Code 1974 § 301 (10 day waiting period)). Finally, a premarital agreement is enforceable if enforcement would not have been unconscionable at the time the agreement was executed (cf. *Hartz v. Hartz*, 234 A.2d 865 (Md. 1967) (premarital agreement upheld if no disclosure but agreement was fair and equitable under the circumstances)).

The test of "unconscionability" is drawn from Section 306 of the Uniform Marriage and Divorce Act (UMDA) (see *Ferry v. Ferry*, 586 S.W. 2d 782 (Mo. 1979); see also *Newman v. Newman*, 653 P.2d 728 (Colo. Sup. Ct. 1982) (maintenance provisions of premarital agreement tested for unconscionability at time of marriage termination)). The following discussion set forth in the Commissioner's Note to Section 306 of the UMDA is equally appropriate here:

"Subsection (b) undergirds the freedom allowed the parties by making clear that the terms of the agreement respecting maintenance and property disposition are binding upon the court unless those terms are found to be unconscionable. The standard of unconscionability is used in commercial law, where its meaning includes protection against onesidedness, oppression, or unfair surprise (see section 2-302, Uniform Commercial Code), and in contract law, Scott v. U.S., 12 Wall (U.S.) 443 (1870) ('contract . . . unreasonable and unconscionable but not void for fraud'); Stiefler v. McCullough, 174 N.E. 823, 97 Ind.App. 123 (1931); Terre Haute Cooperage v. Branscome, 35 So.2d 537, 203 Miss. 493 (1948); Carter v. Boone County Trust Co., 92 S.W. 2d 647, 338 Mo. 629 (1936). It has been used in cases respecting divorce settlements or awards. Bell v. Bell, 371 P.2d 773, 150 Colo. 174 (1962) ('this division of property is manifestly unfair, inequitable and unconscionable'). Hence the act does not introduce a novel standard unknown to the law. In the context of negotiations between spouses as to the financial incidents of their marriage, the standard includes protection against overreaching, concealment of assets, and sharp dealing not consistent with the obligations of marital partners to deal fairly with each other.

"In order to determine whether the agreement is unconscionable, the court may look to the economic circumstances of the parties resulting from the agreement, and any other relevant evidence such as the conditions under which the agreement was made, including the knowledge of the other party. If the court finds the agreement not unconscionable, its terms respecting property division and maintenance may not be altered by the court at the hearing." (Commissioner's Note, Sec. 306, Uniform Marriage and Divorce Act.)

Nothing in Section 6 makes the absence of assistance of independent legal counsel a condition for the unenforceability of a premarital agreement. However, lack of that assistance may well be a factor in determining whether the conditions stated in Section 6 may have existed (see, e.g., *Del Vecchio v. Del Vecchio*, 143 So.2d 17 (Fla. 1962)).

Even if the conditions stated in subsection (a) are not proven, if a provision of a premarital agreement modifies or eliminates spousal support, subsection (b) authorizes a court to provide very limited relief to a party who would otherwise be eligible for public welfare (see, e.g., *Osborne v. Osborne*, 428 N.E. 2d 810 (Mass. 1981) (dictum); *Unander v. Unander*, 506 P.2d 719 (Ore. 1973) (dictum)).

No special provision is made for enforcement of provisions of a premarital agreement relating to personal rights and obligations. However, a premarital agreement is a contract and these provisions may be enforced to the extent that they are enforceable are under otherwise applicable law (see *Avitzur v. Avitzur*, 459 N.Y.S. 2d 572 (Ct. App.).

Section 6 is framed in a manner to require the party who alleges that a premarital agreement is not enforceable to bear the burden of proof as to that allegation. The statutory law conflicts on the issue of where the burden of proof lies (contrast Ark. Stats.

§ 55-313; 31 Minn. Stats. Ann. § 519.11 with Vernon's Texas Codes Ann. § 5.45). Similarly, some courts have placed the burden on the attacking spouse to prove the invalidity of the agreement. *Linker v. Linker*, 470 P.2d 921 (Colo. 1970); *Matter of Estate of Benker*, 296 N.W. 2d 167 (Mich. App. 1980); *In re Kauffmann's Estate*, 171 A.2d 48 (Pa. 1961). Some have placed the burden upon those relying upon the agreement to prove its validity. *Hartz v. Hartz*, 234 A.2d 865 (Md. 1967). Finally, several have adopted a middle ground by stating that a premarital agreement is presumptively valid but if a disproportionate disposition is made for the wife, the husband bears the burden of proof of showing adequate disclosure. (*Del Vecchio v. Del Vecchio*, 143 So.2d 17 (Fla. 1962); *Christians v. Christians*, 44 N.W.2d 431 (Iowa 1950); *In re Neis' Estate*, 225 P.2d 110 (Kans. 1950); *Truitt v. Truitt's Adm'r*, 162 S.W. 2d 31 (Ky. 1942); *In re Estate of Strickland*, 149 N.W. 2d 344 (Neb. 1967); *Kosik v. George*, 452 P.2d 560 (Or. 1969); *Friedlander v. Friedlander*, 494 P.2d 208 (Wash. 1972).

SECTION 7. ENFORCEMENT: VOID MARRIAGE. If a marriage is determined to be void, an agreement that would otherwise have been a premarital agreement is enforceable only to the extent necessary to avoid an inequitable result.

Comment

Under this section a void marriage does not completely invalidate an premarital agreement but does substantially limit its enforceability. Where parties have married and lived together for a substantial period of time and one or both have relied on the existence of a premarital agreement, the failure to enforce the agreement may well be inequitable. This section, accordingly, provides the court discretion to enforce the agreement to the extent necessary to avoid the inequitable result (see Annot., 46 A.L.R. 3d 1403).

SECTION 8. LIMITATION OF ACTIONS. Any statute of limitations applicable to an action asserting a claim for relief under a premarital agreement is tolled during the marriage of the parties to the agreement. However, equitable defenses limiting the time for enforcement, including laches and estoppel, are available to either party.

Comment

In order to avoid the potentially disruptive effect of compelling litigation between the spouses in order to escape the running of an applicable statute of limitations, Section 8 tolls any applicable statute during the marriage of the parties (contrast *Dykema v. Dykema*, 412 N.E. 2d 13 (Ill. App. 1980) (statute of limitations not tolled where fraud not adequately pleaded, hence premarital agreement enforced at death)). However, a party is not completely free to sit on his or her rights because the section does preserve certain equitable defenses.

SECTION 9. APPLICATION AND CONSTRUCTION. This [Act] shall be applied and construed to effectuate its general purpose to make uniform the law with respect to the subject of this [Act] among states enacting it.

Comment

Section 9 is a standard provision in all Uniform Acts.

SECTION 10. SHORT TITLE. This [Act] may be cited as the Uniform Premarital Agreement Act.

Comment

This is the customary "short title" clause, which may be placed in that order in the bill for enactment as the legislative practice of the state prescribes.

SECTION 11. SEVERABILITY. If any provision of this [Act] or its application to any person or circumstance is held invalid, the invalidity does not affect other provisions or applications of this [Act] which can be given effect without the invalid provision or application, and to this end the provisions of this [Act] are severable.

Comment

Section 11 is a standard provision included in certain Uniform Acts.

SECTION 12. TIME OF TAKING EFFECT. This [Act] takes effect _____ and applies to any premarital agreement executed on or after that date.

SECTION 13. REPEAL. The following acts and parts of acts are repealed:

29993421R00094

Made in the USA
Lexington, KY
14 February 2014